Hurricane Blues

Poems about Katrina and Rita

Hurricane Blues

Poems about Katrina and Rita

Editors: Philip C. Kolin and Susan Swartwout

Southeast Missouri State University Press • 2006

Hurricane Blues: Poems about Katrina and Rita

Copyright 2006

ISBN-10: 0-9760413-5-9
ISBN-13: 978-0-9760413-5-1

First published in the United States of America in 2006:

Southeast Missouri State University Press
MS 2650, One University Plaza
Cape Girardeau, MO 63701

http://www6.semo.edu/universitypress

Opinions published herein are not necessarily the views of the editors
nor of Southeast Missouri State University.

Editors: Philip C. Kolin and Susan Swartwout

Cover design by Liz Lester

To all those who suffered

from Hurricanes Katrina and Rita

Table of Contents

Landing

City Under Siege, Under Water

Aftermath

Mourning

Resolutions

Introduction

You came here for a reason.

Perhaps you've picked up this book because you have family or friends who were endangered by Katrina and Rita, hurricanes that devastated the Gulf Coast in 2005. Perhaps you were there, or you've never left. You might be looking for new insights and images of the tragedy, explanations of how and why it happened, as well as how and why the devastation continues.

Whatever your reason, you're holding a unique artifact of American history: an anthology of original poems about the two most infamous hurricanes of 2005. One of them was the most catastrophic in American history. Many of these poems are eyewitness accounts—written by both distinguished and emerging poets, all of whom were moved by the destruction of a legendary American city and the roughly 300-mile radius within Katrina's wrath. The Gulf Coast disaster must not be lost in time. Its emotional and physical impact must be documented.

We want this collection not only to record history but to serve in some way as a balm, a relief effort toward the inevitable reconstruction of the region. Accordingly, all proceeds from *Hurricane Blues* will go toward the relief effort. This is poetry as bread, cast upon the surface of the waters.

Why poetry? Poetry's truthfulness and visionary qualities, its ability to convey emotion as well as information, belong to everyone. William Carlos Williams in his poem "Asphodel, That Greeny Flower" explains that poetry must avoid being seen as only a secret language of poets. Rather, it must also locate itself in issues of the public at large, in what "concerns many." While the poems in *Hurricane Blues* are of, by, and for the people, that's only half their battle. Poetry must also put us at risk, make us uncomfortable in its observations of life on this planet. Through poetry's observations, changes may and should be made, so that the human spirit may be uplifted and balanced. At the end of "Asphodel," Williams profoundly declares that "it is difficult / to get the news from poems / yet men die miserably every day / for lack of what is found there."

Some readers will likely be made uncomfortable by what they find here, but we must remember such events in order not to repeat them—remember them not simply as acts of nature, which we do not control, but as disasters of assumption, neglect, and ignorance, which we do. Poetry emblazons such imagery on the national consciousness. Ezra Pound affirmed that nations will be judged by their anthologies.

In her essay, "Blood, Bread, and Poetry: The Location of the Poet," Adrienne Rich explains that we fear poetry, because "it might get to [society] on a level we have lost touch with, undermine the safety we have built for ourselves, remind us of what is better left forgotten." The poems in *Hurricane Blues* are meant to keep the tragedies of Katrina and Rita in our minds and hearts, and thus can help us to be better prepared to face other natural disasters.

We must also remember and be prepared because much of what happened could have been prevented and should have been, as many of these poems inform us. Just three weeks before John F. Kennedy's assassination, he gave a speech entitled "The Purpose of Poetry" to honor Robert Frost. In it, he reminds us, "When power corrupts, poetry cleanses, for art establishes the basic human truths which must serve as the touchstones of our judgment." Katrina's cleansing will require vigilance and truthseeking by us all.

Hurricane Blues is dedicated to such a quest. Katrina, with its 140 mph winds, is billed as "the most devastating natural disaster in U.S. history," triggering a diaspora that surpasses any other in American memory. Thousands died; 1.3 million people were evacuated; 20,000–25,000 people were left behind for days in horrific conditions of filth and brutality at the Superdome and the Convention Center in New Orleans; 600,000 homes were hit, making them uninhabitable; 200,000 cars were destroyed under water or from the wind, fallen trees, mountains of displaced sand; and the clean-up bill exceeds billions, with a completion date of at least ten years, according to President George W. Bush. Even a year after the storm, dead bodies are still being found inside houses, under bridges; boats are still ensnared in treetops.

But Katrina was more than a natural disaster. As Susan Jean Jackson, the spokesperson for the Army Corps of Engineers, concluded, "It is like *Apocalypse Now*." Katrina is the zeitgeist of the first decade of the 21st century. Her name—"Evil wind"—is an ominous harbinger, and for many, Katrina in fact brought doomsday to the Gulf South on that last Monday in August. "We're facing the storm most of us have feared," said New Orleans Mayor Ray Nagin in the *Times-Picayune*. "This is going to be an unprecedented event."

Katrina spawned human-generated woes as well. The hurricane unleashed revolution in the flooded streets and on the screens of high definition TVs. Victims stranded in trees, over bridges, and on rooftops— holding signs that said "Pleas help"—ignited raw political rhetoric, intensifying the chorus of charges against incompetent bureaucrats in Washington, Baton Rouge, New Orleans, the levee board, and a host of parish pariahs who did not do what they were bound under oath to do. A story in *U.S. News & World Report* for June 5, 2006, could state without the slightest fear of opposition: "Officials are only now uncovering the depth of ineptitude displayed at the Homeland Security Operations Center."

Chaos owned the city. Outdoor jails were constructed to hold rioters who defied curfews to rape and to murder as well as looters who stole drugs and supplies from hospitals, TV sets, microwaves, and Reeboks. Troops were brought in to assist police in the Big Easy, prompting the commanding general, Russel Honoré, to declare: "These are Americans. This is not Iraq." Without light, gas, food, even fresh water, the Katrina-hit Gulf was indeed a battlefield. Many compared New Orleans and the Mississippi Gulf Coast to a nuclear strike zone. The shootings, the power failures (both electrical and political), the incarceration of thousands in the Superdome and later in the Astrodome made America seem like a country under siege.

Katrina also transformed the American literary landscape. *Hurricane Blues* bears witness to this. No other natural disaster evoked, paradoxically, such fiery and profoundly introspective poetry. Katrina has given poets a unique anatomy lesson about the body politic and the American character of that body. The hurricane gave its name, its terrors, and its anger to a new canon of American poetry and a new sense of national responsibility for rebuilding and restoring. The images that the poets record in *Hurricane Blues* form their stunning art. Appropriate to the mission of *Hurricane Blues* are the words John F. Kennedy again used in concluding his tribute to Frost, words that reach through the decades to us:

16

I look forward to an America which will not be afraid of grace or beauty, which will protect the beauty of our natural environment, which will preserve the great old American houses and squares and parks of our national past, and which will build handsome and balanced cities for our future.

"Balanced cities" is a post-Katrina hope, dream, and prayer for all those who call New Orleans their physical, literary, or spiritual home.

May *Hurricane Blues* remain bread on the surface of the waters and on the surface of memory, defining the terror and preserving the triumph of a nation.

—PCK and SS

Prelude

Darby Diane Beattie

Memories of Katrina

> *I am 62 years old, life has been good to me,*
> *and I am so glad to be alive.*

I rode out the storm; no money or transportation to leave New Orleans. Katrina made landfall August 29, 2005. The winds' fury took my kitchen walls and blew out the roof from my Napoleon Avenue apartment uptown. The winds howled nonstop in the total darkness. Rain poured like a broken water main, pulled the drains off the roof. It was humid and 100 degrees as I lay on the floor under a boxspring all night long—no sleep, no food, no water. Morning was no relief; the winds and rain stayed on until 3 PM.

Outside, the apartment was covered with uprooted trees. The balcony hung off the building. The street looked like a science fiction war zone. People were desperate for water. No one had any utilities. A nearby swimming pool was blocked by fallen walls and pump equipment, but I climbed a wall to salvage water in a plastic bucket. No sign of help until two days after the storm, when streams of helicopters from the Coast Guard headed for the drowning pools of the City. There was no help from the local police. Local politicians and civic leaders were nonexistant.

I struggled through the front gates to see if I could help anyone. People were milling in the heat, looking for food and water. Children were scared and cried for water. There was no food until the fifth day.

On the fifth day, the first evacuations to the Superdome occurred. The National Guard gave us military rations and patrolled the streets with weapons. Desperation led to looting. The evacuation caused panic in the masses of people. I tried to walk there, but there was too much water still and dangerous heat for that distance. I went back to the apartment.

The military meals were edible and provided nutrition. I ate one each day, waiting for rescue. I felt like a refugee from a far country, not an American. Desperate people, senior citizens, were dying from dehydration. The stench of death was overwhelming and inescapable. I didn't want to die there.

On the eighth day, the National Guard units came door to door. They used trucks to move us to the Convention Center, then helicopters to get us on an airflight out of New Orleans. The pilot wouldn't tell us where we were going until we were en route. Then he announced to some eighty homeless survivors that the U.S. Government was sending us to sunny Tucson, Arizona. I thought, *At least there is no levee there.*

Writing keeps me sane; I write every day. I thank God for the good people of Tucson and their welcome to me. I am 62 years old. A Katrina survivor.

Looming

The Flood, 2005

When Noah prepared his ark
he had precise instructions from above:
so many ribs of cyprus covered with reeds, so many portholes and doors
and where to place them. He was told how to choose the animals—the
pair of ostriches trying to hide their heads, the hummingbirds hovering
over the cardinals' red wings, pigs and camels—all the species already
invented or continuing to evolve.

The rain started slowly: a mist,
a drizzle—drumbeats in the distance becoming a roar, a world, a very
universe of water, and in those stormy howls Noah discerned the cadence
of punishment.
At the end, God's temper blew itself out in a final furious burst of wind,
and the dove was sent to find dry land, the sun returned as if it had
simply taken some casual detour. God went about his usual business

somewhere else.
Who worried about the children,
still stranded on their failing rooftops; the abandoned animals who didn't
make it to the ark; the way so many deaths seemed an almost incidental
part of the story?
Did anyone give instructions
from above, and when?
And if there was sin involved,
wasn't it miles north of the Delta?

Before the Storm

Disappointing weather
forecasters and local news
dollies who love those shots
of horizontal rain to rally
torpid viewers, Odette
balks at moving inland, stalls
in the Gulf like a diva
prolonging her applause.
At dusk the insect chorus
of sodium vapor streetlamps
begins palpitating unevenly on,
backlights the particulate
skim milk haze of humidity
and carbon monoxide.
Against this scrim the tired,
mostly illegal, housecleaners
and dishwashers waiting
for the bus seem like a string
of valedictory performances.
The stars are unrewarding.
Though Orion hunts low
on the horizon, the largest
constellation in this piece
of Houston sky is the King
Mattress neon, its blue cushion,
bilious gold and red crown,
now staining an all-night gas
station's asphalt lot
where I watch from the great,
sickening distance opened
by fear as one man beats another
to the ground. His armpit red
when the shoulder swings
the arm down, the asterism
of his rodeo buckle gleams.

His right knee bent
for leverage burns blue-white
above a nebula of dust,
his face a fist of dark space.

Bar Eye Storm

The width of his steps could hardly take over his own pace
the city sky razor-edged between girders
from curb to curb the echoing of cobble stones—
his shoes resound the earth's gravity five feet below sea level.
In the opening door of a dive
wide spaces between neon beer signs and green pool tables,
his steps extend entering the blue hazed room:
voices, mouthless,
movements of bodies,
black light drapes tan skins in slow satin
eyes are eyes in planets of pupils over the great eclipse of the ceiling
    moving star targets.
To sit at the bar reconciles being alone in solitude, solitary among loners.
It is said power isolates as some say money corrupts.
I read Napoleon was likely color blind
fields of green turned fields of red he would not have distinguished.
The thoughts of a solitary man follow the syntax of his moods,
elliptical and tangential,
something of a climate, transient sea elements restitute into present,
happiness, or resentment—
a moon in his hat.
Glimmers above the bar catch over the *comptoir*
words and liquors breathe on the tongue
take to the brain,
return into air diminishing spaces between loners.
Somebody says—we are under watched,
meaning the hurricane
Katrina still offshore
ghastly foam eye
dead center inside a tepid beer glass.

After Tropical Storm Cindy

The banana trees in the backyard are bent
and broken. I had plans for their
apple custard fruit. Too early in the season,
too green, even if I left them in the sun
to yellow; all skin, no pulp, I throw them on
the garbage heap. I walk back to the mud hole.
The sweet gum crashed through the iguana
cage. Pretty Baby was fortunate, having
been moved inside earlier in the night.
It took me three days to hand cart all the
destructed scenery to the street for pick up.
A week later and a hurricane scare,
the house is still there and so is the pile
of what was once landscape. Another,
unnamed for the moment, is building steam
in the Atlantic and is projected to enter
the Gulf. I've almost had enough. It's
still July and the forecasters all claim
that this is going to be a very busy season.

The Times-Picayune *as Prophet*

I'd almost forgotten,
  from my years in Gentilly,
  fifteen years ago,
  the series in *The Times-Pic*:
  "Those paranoid lefties,"
  everyone said,
  "trying to stir up trouble."

The reporters said the levee's too low,
    I-10's too low,
    East & West, North & South:
    not enough ways out.
    Those with cars would creep
    through hours of jams,
    and those who were poor
    (too many to count)
    and those who were elderly
    (too insignificant to count)
    would have to find buses
    to get themselves out.
    If the rains came,
    if the winds blew
    at certain angles,
    the bowl would fill,
    changing life forever.

I remembered that series
  as September was dawning
  and I was dialing my aunt
  who was huddled in damp, dark silence.
  I heard the recording that looped
  "the network is down"
  and I lamented the green-palmed petty politicians
  who spoke on behalf
  of the poor and the elderly

at the time of election
but failed to plan
for the time of destruction.

Remembering the series, I realized
The Times-Pic had been like Noah of old,
warning of the coming flood
for so many years
the neighbors had said
he was crazy and ignorant,
haunted by phantom fears.
And I pondered the mystery
of how hard it is
to discern between prophecy and paranoia
'til the flood finally comes
and vindicates the alarmist prophet.

Big Wheel Keeps On Turning

("Proud Mary," Credence Clearwater Revival)

—for Shanna and James

On the Way Out

I can tell she wants to be told.

I know the kind of trouble that brings.

Tell her and she'll do it.

I'm not ready to be that wrong.

Apologies always deep and dark as coal.

For six or seven days, weather hysteria

has been ramping up. The thrill

of destruction close to all our hearts.

A challenge to each of our imaginations.

To go or not to go? I say wait

another day and hang up the phone.

Next day the evacuation is made mandatory.

She begins to stuff her car

like a Thanksgiving turkey.

Instead of sage, CD's; instead of turmeric,

books; instead of celery, a photo album;

instead of bread crumbs, unwashed clothes.

An unfamiliar recipe that's been handed down

for thousands of years: exodus, diaspora,

the vocabulary always expanding—refugee,

displaced person, evacuee. Never a good cook,

a turkey might have more room

than her arthritic Volkswagon

with 290,000 miles—she's made it

to the moon and back with a couple

of trips around the earth thrown in.

At least the odometer still works.

She drives across the parish in the rain

to where her boyfriend lives.

He's never owned a car,

doesn't know how to drive.

His cat sits caged in the back seat.

Four hundred miles away,

the transmission succumbs

to a hurricane of exhaustion.

Shahid Devastates Louisiana

My friend wants to be a hurricane,
the type of pressure cooker weather
that savages an oceanfront cliff
into fertilizer and tosses houses
like sleeves of vapor into the black
velvet of galactic space. He wants
people to huddle in the disquiet
of housedark through uncertain,
mystifying hours of listening to the news,
wondering if and when to make
a break for it, and to where. . .
I understand this impulse to be unignored—
my father said when I was little,
I threw up Cheerios on purpose
and wet my pants just to wear epaulets
of my mother's sympathy, so white and free.
I remember being eight years old
in Mrs. Minson's class, and she told us
about the Cold War menace, how any second
of any day of any hour at all, IT could come,
so we'd practice, kneel with heads buried
between knees, waiting for the detonation,
the flood of sound that will shatter the silence
at the hall's fluted throat, our open mouths.
Surely this is what Shahid wants, so many
expectant souls like an echo waiting for the boom.

Jen Karetnick

How to Shop for a Hurricane

—on the eve of landfall

What you'll need depends on whose name is used:
Andrew might require avoidance but
Wilma, maybe denial will do. It's
wait and see what's in store, so don't confuse
the issues. What you'll need does not have to
do with water, batteries, and bleach is
recommended no longer (though candles
—white Shabbat wax is the best to burn slow—
should be enough to last the suffering
of weeks). Truth? You can't find what you'll need
on the shelves by the end of the season;
it's not as specific as you might think.
What you'll need in the end is what you had,
and nothing so simple as a reason.

Rita

Just a damn bunch of water
growls my Desert Storm vet neighbor
as he stubs out a half-done cigar

against his boot heel, but I
am more concerned, having
seen Illinois twisters toss

full-grown Guernseys ninety feet
and crush silos like a crackhead titan.
Within hours, my koi do backflips

on the grass, the backyard pond
exploding up the ridge, against the house,
the back stoop I'd been meaning to waterseal.

The sump pump churns louder
downstairs, and I'm stacking pots,
pans, anything to catch potential

ceiling leaks. My neighbor? Shirtless
on his front porch, scraping off two days'
stubble with a knife that glints

like a moonbeam with each thundercrack.

What the Waters Said

Almost from the beginning
You degraded us into your own image:
That giant's body with
Rocks for bones, earth for flesh,
Forests for hair. But at least
You honored what you could touch.
You trusted the evidence of your senses.
At least, because you understood so little,
Our every act was a miracle
And you knew better
Than to twist the tail of the wondrous.
Before simile and metaphor
Colonized the world,
You recognized us for what we are:
The thisness of your lives.

You took a wrong turn
When you stopped respecting us—
Water, earth, air, fire.
Druids worshipping the oak
Came closer to the nub.
Anthropomorphizing
The universe is arrogant.

Here is the truth:
First we were.
Then men.
Then gods.
Then men as gods
Worshipped by their mortal creators
And accorded agency.
Man-gods from Gilgamesh to Jesus
Were a perilous transition
To who you are now:
Deluded subduers of our world.

Remember:
Although your salvation
Depends upon loving Nature
Nature does not love you.

Remember:
Reading this, you grasp
At personification.
We are not speaking to you.
We have no voice.
We are not gods
Or their tools.
We are. We act.
Our message is molecular.
Build your little levees.
We will rest behind them
Until it pleases us
To do otherwise.

Distant Predictions

All maps and calibrations warn
of more disaster to come.
But from where I sit far north
with my mocha latte and genuine
New Orleans beignet, I'm free
to play with the TV screen's images,
as if they were frames from a deep noir
avant-garde film.

> *Too bad*, says the waitress, *glad*
> *I don't live there. Got to be crazy*
> *to go there*, a man at the next table says,
> *all those sinners and wackos,*
> *The Lord knows they deserve it.*
> *A pity, what a pity*, a woman adds,
> returns to her *Wall Street Journal*.

And I return to my book. But wait!
Who are all those dark
and desolate people shouting from
rooftops and spilling into the
fetid water, never knew
there were so many, must be the spliced
scenes from *The Birth of a Nation*.
But those people look real, almost
my neighbors—but not quite.

Why keep watching.
          My own scenario
          takes place in the French Quarter
where Satchmo and Josephine Baker
          sing a duet re deux amours
                    and a purple-robed rhabdomantist
douses for bourbon, his wand silvery
                    as a distant saxophone
Another latte and a muffuletta, si-vous plait?

Virginia Ramus

Ten Days and Two Thousand Miles

Falling sun has bruised the horizon
    northeast of Hurricane Katrina
        where the Cape May Peninsula
    bends west
around the lighthouse.

Atlantic waters lift,   roll,
    strew silver
      across foot-ruffled sand.
          Wind lays flat the stars
             and stripes lurching upward
        from half-mast for the late Chief
             Justice, then
        slowly down the pole
      to the two hands
    of a vet from one
  war, his face
reverent beneath a blue
Phillies ball cap.

Feeble waves of "God
    Bless America" spray the boardwalk
      from a box on a telephone pole,
        while sunburned boomers
      contort their lips somewhere
    between singing
      and not singing.
Bodies
    from Biloxi and New
                Orleans wash far
      from this New
        Jersey beach.

Right hands leave
       t-shirted chests; sneakers amble
                    off for soft
               ice cream, soft
            beds, ocean darkening
         beneath fingernail
moon visible from all
     over the nation.

In Wisconsin, Hardly a Breeze

Early September. Convulsive illumination
of southwestern clouds, so distant you'd
mistake it for heat lightning if it weren't
for the thunder, muted and lacking resonance,
wooden report like a barn door slamming.

Hardly even a breeze here. A subdued
insect drone seeps up from dark roots of earth.
Late night radio stations a-jump with
Dixieland, zydeco, blues, delta of
the ear backwashed upriver by Katrina.

It's a jazz funeral second-lining
through the streets inside everyone now,
flood flotsam of America's psyche. New
Orleans, hold on, don't let go! How would our
heart beat without the city that birthed Satchmo?

Landing

Sorry

All night the trees keep saying the same thing
over and over: *Sorry*.
Sorry. Sorry. They're embarrassed by their leaves'
limited vocabulary, their roots'
squalor. The whole world's sorry tonight.
A man lets the room grow dark
around him and writes this one word
again and again. *Sorry*
As if his shock at what had happened
could make it any less terrible. As if the air cared.
As if the shadows had the slightest interest
in anyone's suffering. *Sorry*.
As if feeling bad ought to count for something.
Sorry. As if horror had to serve some purpose.
Sorry. Sorry. All night
the trees apologize too. *Sorry*.
They know it makes nothing right.
They say it anyway.

Jianqing Zheng

The Katrina Dance

When Katrina is approaching,
the giant oaks around our house begin to
shake like belly dancers

while the wind chimes hanging
from the porch ceiling jingle like anklets.
In a moment they wobble lightheartedly

like the Canada geese around the edge of
a fishpond in the Mississippi Delta,
honking like wind-lovers in a low voice.

Then they foxtrot or waltz
in gentle rise and fall,
spin turns with stylish breaks.

Hours later, as Katrina swashes by,
they lurch in tipsy steps as if having drunk
too much of the strong wind.

They grow wild now.
Their long sleeves sway, their bodies
tremble and bend in all directions.

They begin to dismantle.
Leaves swirl in warm rain, limbs snap and
drop on the roof and ground.

Then power is gone and the oaks
become ghostlike. They dance wildly
in darkness, freely expressing themselves.

Fingers-crossed, my wife and I
keep praying to the trees:
Don't fall; don't fall.

Storm Surge

As the floodwaters of blood
receded in my wife's brain, the Gulf
engulfed the streets of her hometown.
How odd to be stranded across the sea
while watching on TV the stranded
on overpasses and in the ruptured Superdome.
Grand Isle, where we fished the surf,
nearly washed away, like the sands
beneath our feet in Wales.
What home could we go home to?
Email from high school classmates told
how parents and friends were safe, lost, or still unheard from, though
we knew exactly where we were, Intensive Care, but at least alive, not
floating face down in a bayou or back street. Bad as it was, she woke
up, against the experts' odds, and the city, too, proved tougher than the
pundits, already planning another Mardi Gras, Papa Noelle, Jazz Fest
with its tubs of gumbo, all of us rising to fais do do
into the future.

Sue Walker

Mother Nature Gone Wild

She was no lady but a tramp,
a traveler up to no good,
screaming, ranting,
and leaving fury
in her wake. She was the devil's
raging grandma, Katrina,
her mouth pursed in the kiss of death.

Some thought she wouldn't lash out
at them—oh no. And they'd deal
with what the dame dished out.
They'd known the Galewind family's wrath
before, knew her crazy aunt Camille,
knew her no-count cousin Frederick.

Then when Katrina started acting mad
as a pig on ice, they never dreamed
she'd take it out on children, but Ma Nature
went wild. Wild as a wyvern,
that two-legged dragon with a snake
on its ass.

When she'd gone, and the waning moon
hid its face, those left behind
had more to do than mourn.
They climbed into attics,
sat on rooftops, and measured
countless hours as they cooked
in the sun. No water to drink,
nowhere to run, they died.

Bodies floated in stagnant waters.
Grown men wept. One man said
he held out his hand to his wife,
but her fingers slipped. She couldn't hold on.

"What will you do?" someone asked,
and he cried: "I'm lost. Don't have no place to go."

But the question is: who can go home again
when acres of marshland have vanished,
when Louisiana's shoreline's destroyed,
and the Pres can't bring himself
to speak "Wetlands" or "Barrier Islands,"
and doesn't understand about Ma Nature,
peril and response, indeed doesn't know
"consilience," know that abusing the Mother
Earth, cutting 8,000 miles of canals
like a maze disfiguring her face
will raise her wrath
and make her storm again,
again.

Water Table

My parents live on stilts.
The table propped up on bricks
the good chairs on top the table
the lesser chairs in various states of decay.

Every since the flood of eighty nine
they got tired of picking up and putting down.
Every thing stays up
that isn't in use every day.

When the flood of ninety seven came
we picked up what was still down
the rice can, the books on the lower shelf,
the shoes, suitcases and mother's sewing box.

The water knew our plan.
It sneaked in while we slept,
a little dew around the baseboard
a few drips at the window.

Then the rain knocked on the doors,
the wind opened the shutters;
all came in uninvited and took up
residence like scavenger dogs.

We woke to find the river
sitting at table ready to lap up all we had.
Mom didn't scream for the mop,
she was already defeated.

Dad asked for coffee
we stared bleakly. He said,
"This is Ascension Parish,
our yard was once a rice paddy."

We sat in the lesser chairs,
drank black coffee and ate cold bread
while sloshing our booted feet in
muddy water up to the knee.

We remembered all the other floods,
the ones that destroyed our picture perfect
dreams and left us with peeling walls
and curling baseboards.

The time brother dove in and landed
on a floating ant hill.
Mom greased him with Vaseline
and held him till he fell asleep

dreaming of ants and floating garden snakes.
We sloshed in water all day
inventing new kingdoms
and pretending we had a backyard pool.

Daddy had to load us in the boat
and row us to the road to catch the school bus.
We remembered the flood of eighty three
when Dad refused to leave for shelter.

He had ten new pigs and vowed to go down
holding them on the last island of land.
He would sit home through every flood.
Keeping the fort in his old *Lazy Boy* chair.

Tenements

In humid climates where heavy rain takes root,
Tenements gut & bleed, crayfish run

Under front porches. What brute
Force cannot dislodge, days of rain

Easily wash away. Unpainted fruit
Has fallen, is falling, going, going, gone.

Backwater tenements, never proud, are put
To shame, laid to rest by a hurricane's

Goatish head, growing fleece & horns to butt
Down the heaviest doors. Most common pine

Gives way, & what was tightly shut
Is now wide open; floors become lanes

For salt & filth. To put down foot
Is to drown, no planks to float upon,

No easy swimming. Beaches that recruit
Tourists spit sand into our drains,

Clog pipes, bury every feeble shoot
Underfoot. Over sea surge & swell, sun

Finally breaks thru; wind dances about
Hundreds dead, dances over what remains.

Hurricane Kwame Offers His Two Cents

My cousin Katrina just twist-whipped the Big Easy.
She wanted to see how stone-cold bitch she could be.
You know us hurricanes don't start off as giant
funnel cakes rolling houses and trees in sweet death.
We're usually just some restless stirrings
rustling waves like fluffy baby locks
blowing across the Atlantic's head.
You could say our rotating relatives
were Africans, born on the continental coast.
Of course, our cousins from the Pacific come
mostly from South America & Mexico, but
those Olmec heads look a lot like faces back home.
She can't front that they were making too much
zydeco/jazz rumbling saturated with gin and hoodoo.
Even God understands a party every now and then.
All them loas just like Jesus.
Those reverends preaching cleansing have no idea
how close hurricanes curl toward the ears of God.
In fact, my girl Rita decided to visit Texas just to rattle the faith
of that president boy's skull, especially since you know that brain
clatters around like a mess of dried beans. These journalists lack
just as much sense talking about people looting,
well hell, I must be one of Nature's looters snatching
from whatever these newspapers call Civilization.
Ain't it human nature to eat, drink water, and diaper a baby?
At least one journalist got it right though, spelled
my name correct and e'rything. He said this Hurricane
should have been called Kwame or Keisha, but still,
I'm not so sure that was a compliment, since some
hold African names they don't like
so tight in their jaw, you'd think someone still
made up names for chattel, like unmarked
graves wishing that the family bible remembered them.

Elegy in Thirteen Winds

Hollywood Beach, Florida

She arrived all at once, everywhere.

She fell on West coast, East coast, down past Key West, up to Port St. Lucie—

Now her memory is communal, like sucking.

We slept for an hour in her blind iris. A sparrow came to the feeder, which swung then snapped when the wind blinked.

We hunkered in the tub until the back of the eye wall, laughing at shutters, passed.

We got on the phone later and said: Remember, it was 10:30 and we thought the windows were coming in?

Communal as blue jeans.

There was a curtain rod with café curtains stuck under the wheel of my car as if I'd driven onto it.

Cars made pyramids.

Glass in the streets. Glass in the mouth. Sand in the glove compartment. Sand in the cat's ear.

The Diane Motel lost its roof and its vowels.

I kept myself from collecting letters from all over the beach for this poem.

City Under Siege, Under Water

Nicole Cooley

New Orleans Triptych

1.
On TV, the president stands in the dark city in his own private
circle of light, in a cornflower blue work shirt.

The president stands under Klieg lights, under the shadow
of the statue of Andrew Jackson.

The president stands safely center stage, loss off to the left, or the right.

> Stage left: here is a woman and her two children
> who have climbed onto an attic roof,
> perpetually awaiting rescue.

> Stage right: with what has been described
> as a loud cracking, as an explosion,
> the breach occurs, over and over,

2.
The poem is a reading of _____.

The poem is a misreading. The poem is. Misreading.

How to read the breach. How to read an emptied city.

On my desk miles away a snow globe of Jackson Square
I collected as a child
empty once was filled with water

3.
At my kitchen table, miles away, my mother
draws a map of the levees on my daughters'

orange construction paper. Daughters who
are linked to that landscape but don't know it.

Who don't remember ever visiting this city.
With a crayon my mother sketches the edge:

The Gulf. The Lake. East New Orleans. St. Bernard.
Here is the Ninth Ward. Here is Treme. Here are

the canals where the pumps were useless, the workers
already sent out of the city. Here is the river where

we live, where the levee didn't break.
At the kitchen table my daughters sit beside her,

listening. Houses marked X. Houses marked O.
Come for a day, my mother says, alone.

This city is no place for children.

Pavel Chichikov

In the Theater

The angel Death, ahead of me
Climbs up to the balcony—
We sing the Dies Irae, irae—
Not occupied, some seats are free

We sit in our ascending rows—
Projected on the screen below
Apocalypsis soon to show—
When it begins no one may go

The angel wears a garment black,
No light escapes, there is no crack
Admitting future's blazing back
As it advances on its track

The angel Death will not sit down
Or take away his midnight gown
From shoulders wide as Earth around—
The sea's horizon is his crown

Three Modes of Katrina

i: Katrina's Darkness

One might say unnatural; but night, like day, shapes
round our lives and orders them—while reassuring stars,
or sparkling imitations we devise, trace out
designs for us. No stars tonight. Uneasy, then,
for the Big Easy—as, flailed by the hurricane,
it hunches down in utter darkness, with no street lamps

on the Avenue, no glow around the Dome, no rooms
lit brightly for the ones who cannot sleep,
or did not wish to, who had rather read, or brood
in bars, or stake their fates on card games or with women.
And here I am awake with them, though not by choice—
treading in soggy slippers on the tile along the windows,

mopping up water that I feel but cannot see,
wringing out rags to use again, adding old newspapers,
waiting for dawn, when I can see how deep it is,
how far it's soaked the carpet, whether books
along the wall are wet. We'll eat cold food tonight,
heat coffee water by a candle, watch the waves that prance

up Second Street, and wonder when the power
will return. But Paul says, "This is nothing, really."
He is right; it's just a blast of noise as from a boom-box—
drum-rolls, tedious blare, and constant whining—and a bit
of inconvenience. Or so we think; we can't yet know
it's not a rap song, but the overture to *Götterdämmerung*.

ii: Katrina's War

So she was not bluffing, though by Monday afternoon
our streets were nearly clear. True, the trees were tattered,
skeletal, all stripped of limbs and leaves, and water
had collected in the kitchen of an absent friend,
where I went after it with mop and pail. The air
was steamy, but we lasted, innocent, till Tuesday morning.

Meanwhile, storm surge in the lakes has breached,
or topped, the levees; yet the radio (a single station
working in a bunker on the West Bank) tells us
nothing. All we know about is crowds of ill and helpless
gathered in the Superdome—discomfort, thirst
and hunger, crying children, sleeplessness, and fear. Then

the news: the dykes have broken; Poydras and Canal Street
are awash, the water rising, close. *We're* the lucky
ones: my Jeep's not flooded, we've got gasoline
(enough to cross the river, get to New Iberia) and friends
in Texas. *Still*, we do not get it—like a war,
when just a skirmish that should soon be over turns

quite nasty, and the battle lines are drawn, and next,
it's full-scale conflict in the trenches, while the locals,
caught in the cross-fire, barely know what's happening.
We saw the war on television, with another—
young men dying in the desert; old men, women,
dogs and children drowned or on an overpass, abandoned.

iii: Katrina's Gifts

I cannot think like Nagin, who announced*
the storm was sent to punish us for war
abroad and selfishness at home—and thus
I do not purpose to explain such ways
of God to man. But Milton saw things well:
all history is *Sturm und Drang*, the winds

and seas of human action in the world
contending, force and counter-force, the tides
now wildly drowning everything, now drawn
by other moons and falling—whether men
alone contest and struggle, or enroll
the wiles of nature, or invoke divine

intentions. Coming back, we saw the wrath
of Rita first: beheaded pine trees, roofs
wrenched off, debris. And then Katrina's deeds—
swamps stripped, shacks gone, the city's spectral face
reflected in the water. One gives thanks,
however, for such gifts as whirlwinds leave—

not like the Pharisee, self-gratified,
but knowing how precarious is life—
a fragile causeway over turbulence—
as risk and chance conspire in destiny;
so that we grieve, but live in greater love—
good friends, dry bed, a spirit fired white.

---

*Ray Nagin, the New Orleans mayor, in a Martin Luther King, Jr. Day speech,
January 2006.

Peter Cooley

I See a City in Tears

And he said unto me: what do you see?
Then I answered: I see only darkness.
And he said: that will not do. Answer me.
Then I said: I see a city in tears,
abomination of desolation,
bodies of the drowned afloat in back streets,
graves of the dead buried above ground sprung
open and skeletons whole and in pieces
set out to decimate the morning light.
And he said: that is better. But what else?
Then I answered: my words are little, poor.
Why do you persecute me to write this,
I, who lost so little, I who was spared,
who drove home to find his house staring back
with eyes none of which had a single crack
nor was its head to suffer but black rain
rose before him in the blazing noon
unscathed, therefore, why should I try to speak?
And the voice, which will never let me go,
the voice standing beside me in torment,
in jubilation, all my days before,
spoke again, merely repeating: what else?

Elizabeth Foos

How to lose your hometown in seven days

Hometowns aren't good for much, except
knowing them longer than anywhere else,
you know they will take you back
when nowhere else will, and knowing them
longer you know the great dive for cornbread
off 22nd and who used to live in the corner
house and when that road didn't go through,
and you can always find a job or a cheap place
to sleep or an old friend with a back slap
with your name on it or news of nobody
you've thought of in years, and knowing how
to get home from all directions and the numbers
of highways and interstates out to everywhere,
and knowing always knowing it will wait there
like first love and never give up on you, unless—

unless the globe gets hot enough to make monsters
from thin air, twisted and one-eyed and send them
tearing through the streets, cracking power
poles, grabbing trees by the boughs and pushing
them down on anything dumb enough to live
under a water oak or live oak or gone pecan tree
so the whole city can't see or eat and the heat swells
and somewhere down one of those roads you know
the levees kick out and the water starts rising
and there are people everywhere—on couches,
churches, floors, and there's no room at the inns
or the Marriott and there is no bread or milk
or meat and the heat keeps rising
and the streets wrap up and sirens squall all day
into the blackest nights a city's ever seen
and nothing moves until the helicopters
thwup thwup thwup thwup thwup thwup
thwup thwup thwup the silent sky to pieces
so you start raking and thinking of all the other
places you've ever been and how to get there again.

Everywhere, Water

Everywhere, water.
Gasoline-spoiled and
rancid. Borderless,
craving submerged banks.
A hungry water—
erosive, barren,
parasitic drink.

It is full of death.
Life skims the surface,
looking out for more.
But there's only death—
bodies tied to trees,
waterlogged graveyards,
people left behind.

It is not water
anymore; it's a
city's slow bleeding.
Levees buckle like
collapsed arteries.
The Delta's heart is
broken, and beaten.

Graupel

Her words, like soft hail, pepper
the air, her pleas for money in a
dry city disregarded. As the
illiterate winds breech her home's
windows and the streets she
had walked for years flood,
her words create an ice fog that
goes unheard, for she is a black
refugee in a country that once
lynched her forefathers and
now wears an ice cap over its
self-proclaimed principles.
The platitudes still churn
from these clannish props,
who in disgrace, utter clarion
promises, the people of color
whipped purple with a grim
reminder that the fight for
their rights has just begun.

Janet McCann

Katrina Notes

woman in a cage, rising
gray helicopter lifting woman
hair streaming a pennant

mouth open slightly
hands clenched
she is going up, she is flying

away, below her the
rancid flood the bodies the
sounds torn loose from their

meanings, and she rides
over the rooftop her mouth
forming words, a call, a

prayer, for the others
in the water, in the streets,
on the roofs, this her last look

at home, to be what comes back
to her in the knotted sleep
of the rest of her life

after they set her down, not
altogether gently, somewhere
other than here

***

I am trying to learn
the speech of darkness, what I cannot say
it is like but not the same as silence
it is not mine
     to speak
but I cannot look away
waves of people surge

up and down the wasted streets
looting? A grandmother with a loaf of bread,
the mechanical police
closing in like a trap? I would be there, if I were there,
if my heart, my legs had strength to move,
bread in one hand, bottle of water
in the other.

***

grandparents' pictures high on the wall, sepia,
a black-and-white wedding,
children's photos below, there you are
in a red romper.

There is the point to which the water rose,
beneath, a riot of rot, caked mud,
mold crawling up the ruined wall
to the bright pictures of children

who will not be back, who if they live
will go into exile among strangers,
sepia pictures curling
in a deep drawer.

***

In dream I see them again, figures
plucked from roofs,
taken away in baskets by great birds.

Swaths of hair streaming
in wind. Wet, muddy,
carrying nothing,

the way God might take you
to heaven, the way you might
be born, unborn,

blowing hair, hands
gripping the basket—the world,
the whole spoiled world, dropping away.

Watery Ground

The sky above New Orleans indents
where gulls dip down
as if having tripped
into a hole
of vacant air.

Jazzy angels are hip to what isn't there
and the dead tread water
toward Bourbon Street.

Alarm, Set to the News Channel

Your first thought on waking is water-
logged in musty dream closets
punctuated by a narrator who is
reciting the weather as if it
were a math problem.
You step outside the net of sleep
but can't fathom the concepts of ebb
and flow, and what it would be to live
on a roof for five days, taking
small sips from a one-gallon jug,
scanning the sky for wind or rescue
while the city, which has always
carried on so, the city, bold stripper
that she is, up to her eyeballs in filth,
while oily water swirls and shapes
float, bobbing almost beautifully
like a surreal painting, nightmares among
branches, there a doll without her clothes,
and then, refrigerators.

When the Alexandria Quartet Became a Ragtime Band

I. Beneath the Raised Graves

How what we awaited yesterday
Could cause tomorrow to come a cropper,
There's a prediction no one made.

How a wind could uproot our fantasies,
Its waters overflow our channels of command,

Leaving feces and filth to spread a skin condition

We'd swear we had heard claimed cured,

Decades of barrels and barricades
Blocking the bridges,
Democracy derailed,

All gone much further than five hundred miles
When the day was done.

II. All the King's Horses and All the King's Men

I was never in New Orleans
And know that now I'll never be
Since how such a humpty-dumpty city
    Could
    Ever
    Be
    Put
    Together
    Again
Defies the best imaginations.
In the same way you can't make French Provincial

Out of knotty pine;
No Lego look-alike will do.
Or the way a stage of foam and staples
Looks still substantial
Even under the actors' weight,
But wouldn't bring a price on the open market.
Or how water, as the ancients understood,
Is one of the very elements,
At least one of its parts never standing alone,
Like one of two people married for decades will immolate
In preference to abandoning
The dead.
Not like Japan, a mere nation, that could be rebuilt
Because it was only a country,
But like trying to resurrect a perspective our eyes no longer see,
As the discovery of germs
Relegated the hand of God
To the jargon of insurance,
As wonderlands, witches, and wizards
Remain only in fiction and politics,
Like trying to imagine a flat earth from space,
Now, when kings and horses and men, too,
Have become as antiquated as honor,
And all that is left
Are halls of fame.

III. New Orleans Beat Cops: Faces

a.
The sirens sounding in the silence
Seem endless, like the days
Flooding into days, the hours
With no sleep, beat, dead beat.

b.
Standing out there
Between someone and something,
Bereft of everything, spying meager stores
Of food or water. Maddened mobs
Who only want someone to do something

With the dead body on their steps,
Their ax handles and shovels brandished,
Shouting cop. Beat the cop.

c.

Yes, under orders, sure.
With a night stick, a phaser, and cuffs.
Patrolling where they are scrabbling out of the muck,
Scum on the waters
That filled the streets, the stores, the buildings.
A throbbing through my head bidding: Beat.
Beat the bloody bastards away from our bridge.

d.

This is, you know, a pay check.
Like, to be honest, my uncle's wife's sister
From up in Algiers, friends of the Turpins,
And a Turpin one of the officers at precinct,
When my uncle got tired of supporting us
After Dad's accident and set up a job,
And I traded in Beausoleil for a badge,
But it's still cool, man,
Just a beat on the beat, you know?

IV. The Corps of Discovery

It started out
Same old same old. You know the story.
For lack of a brace, the brick wall was lost,
For lack of a wall, the firmament fell,
A kingdom for a horse, even a polo pony.

Not for lack of making a contribution, the labors were lost.

We discovered then that there's no quarter given
When the piper comes for his pay
Made vicious from waiting too long.

Discovered that corruption's too fragile
To stand storm or scrutiny,

A city and its backwater cousins
As flimsy on the front page
As they were in the wind and water.

Discovered that, when the trumpet sounds,
Baby, it isn't always jazzing you.

Some discovered their walkers weren't legal tender
For a ticket out,
Another that a war on poverty had petered out
Into a war on the poor,
While many were busy discovering
They were black after all
And that they had neighbors to tell them
If they'd missed it.

Discovered that when it comes to disaster
Zydeco makes a lousy zeitgeist
And that old world charm
May not soothe the savage beast.

V. Minotaur Among the Metaphors

The screen is filled with fire engines,
Sirens sounding, wheels rumbling
Through the silent streets;
The figure 5, once gold, now measures
What sends our metaphors staggering,
Our minotaur, a bull
Raging through our china shop of metonyms.

What is a roof over your head
When roofs have taken to the air?
Or a foundation under our feet
When nothing any longer holds anything up?

Sashes sashaying through the night sky
Make a mockery of windows of opportunity,
And doors hoisted off their hinges

72

Make you wonder what it is God never shuts
Without opening another.

If this storm in this port,
Then it's no longer any port in a storm.
When the grill-work balconies end up proving
Iron bars do a prison make,
Where then the similes that gave us solace?

Like soldiers surrendering their swords,
We stand before a rain
That fell unduly on the just
And a rainbow that turned out to be
The wolf at the door.

New Orleans (Big Stuff)

for Leonard Bernstein and Billie Holiday

"Play it,"
he says, "however you want,"
and Mr. Christian rides a comet,
bursts the cobalt vault
               somewhere past twilight

as she asks,
"How could you leave me here with all this beauty?"
drowned by the chorus:
"Why is it taking them so *long*?"
amid empty bags of Utz
and memories of okra easing
like an egg
through teeth.

Laying heads so *so* low down
for however else to bear
the weight?

Tattered shadows wave
over a sea of burnt skin
until finally the grand
parade marches
into a terrible swamp
and not much sunset:
sun weary of blinding
with a jarringly slow
goodbye to a paradise
lonely for Louis,
those triumphant shouts
an entirely different fire,
you know, all that long-
gone laughter. Just

say someone will hear us.

Hurricane Katrina

The hurricane eye is shaped as an aborted newborn
according to a Christian television station,
so what was that body floating in the water
diagnosed as pure as raw sewage?
Let the finger pointing begin.

The politicians are more concerned with looting
than rescuing or bottled water or diapers
while the head of a nursing home fled
leaving the patients to fend for themselves.
Let the finger pointing begin.

Lake Pontchartrain was pregnant with water
from years of compassionate cutbacks
as politicians put their fingers in their ears.
If despair was a sandwich, the poor would be well fed.
Let the finger pointing begin.

The storm had the energy of a 10-mega-ton nuclear bomb
exploding every 20 minutes. The coastline had been vanishing
the rate of 33 football fields, letting the accusations flood.
The government knew this day was coming.
Now our fingers are toxic questions.

Last year Senator Landrieu brought 25 children
to the French Quarter, strapped them in Life Jackets,
let them stand on a wrought-iron balcony above blue tarp
representing how high water might reach some day.
Children grasped reality with tight fingers.

Black waters rose to poverty levels
as shafts of biblical lights swarmed through cracks
of the infrastructure of Homeland Insecurity
as the poor asked: where is the exit strategy?
Ah, hell, let the finger pointing begin.

Nicole Cooley

Death of an American City

(italicized text from New York Times *editorial, 12/11/05)*

We are about to lose New Orleans.

An aerial view: too much swamp. Airport empty.

President Bush stood in Jackson Square and said, "There is no way to imagine America without New Orleans."

Elysian Fields: a tangle of trees, cars covered in mud.

At this moment the reconstruction is a rudderless ship.

Armstrong Park: grass gone, ground scabbed.

It all boils down to the levee system.

St. Charles Avenue: streetcar missing, lampposts torn out by the roots

People will clear garbage, live in tents

Lower Ninth: houses marked in the search for bodies, an O, an X.

stalling till the next hurricane season

Lakeview: Oriole Street, Lark Street: "We Tear Down Houses."

leaving nothing but a few shells for tourists to visit like a museum

Mid-City: street after street Blue Roofed.

Total allocations for the wars in Iraq and Afghanistan and the war on terror have topped $300 billion. All that money has been appropriated as the cost of protecting the nation from terrorist attacks. But what was the worst possible case we fought to prevent?

An aerial view: evacuation does not make vacant.

Schools. Neighborhoods. Roads. Electricity and water lines

A new vocabulary. A language no one is willing to speak: Rebuild.
Rebuild. Rebuilt.

Philip C. Kolin

Slaver Superdome

Herded down like
The black sheep
Of Internet America
They were sealed in the belly
Of the slaver Superdome
For the rough passage
Through the privy of
American dreams.

They were kept in chains
By government plutocracy
White-collared stigmas
Booked their torture
On the slaver
Everyone looked like an addict
Hooked on despair
In knee-deep filth.

Against the whipping winds
Spinning politicians' lies
They heard the cries
Of their ancestors in agony
Who erected the levees,
Sowed rice, indigo, cotton, and sorrow
And had their bodies lifted up
As living sacrifices.
They prayed for deliverance
On the fanless gallery
Around St. Louis Cathedral.

This time there was no deliverance
The stench of history smothered compassion.
Federal hearts disconnected in their own chambers.
The white owners didn't even know
The slaver had sailed or how many

Shackled futures were slammed on board.
It was not a place to linger.

Deep down in the hole
They existed on rations of lies,
Slags of hysteria; they drank
The flotsam of anger.

Their nightmares exploded
In the captive air
Swollen with coughs,
Throat-red rage,
Strips of flesh flailing
Like tongues.

Descant helicopters discharged
Messages from phony abolitionists.
Black freedom was jettisoned
Once again over the side—
To accommodate marketplace suspicions.

A slave too old to survive
Died slumped in irons.
Millions of eyes bought the sight
At auctions nationwide
On white plasma TV.

The slaver still sails
Across a sea of agony.
It is rigged again for the journey
In sister and brother ships
Docking in Houston, Detroit, Chicago.
Written on every manifest:
Destiny.

Elizabeth Howard

In Praise of Mourning Doves

They flee hunters' guns,
flock to feeders,
roost in maples,
dust-bathe in the meadow,
their sad, sad song
morning to evening.
We grab binoculars
for buntings and grosbeaks,
but nobody stirs for mourning doves,
part of the landscape,
familiar as stones at forest edge.

Until we hear of New Orleans.
No birds sang after Katrina,
the old black man said.
Dogs howled,
cats squalled,
helicopters whirred,
sirens screamed,
but no birds.
After forty days,
we awoke to birdsong,
mourning doves cooing.
My wife,
too sick to leave
when the hurricane struck,
crawled out of bed and
stood at the broken window.
Water going down, she said.

I pour cracked corn
into the feeder
watch from the porch
as stone-gray birds hover down
like helicopters.

Projection

For close to a week I watched
as the city became water and thousands
huddled on rooftops or jammed into
stadiums, and did nothing.
    I felt like a government.

The Grateful Gratitude Blues

While the politicians drone and the luckless people drown
And the waters come to swallow old New Orleans town
We thank you very kindly yes we thank you Mr Brown

We saw you on the TV set showing what you'd done
How you flew the delta over and waved from Air Force One
It was you and Mr Brown sir yes you and Mr Brown

I've been a long time thinking and it is my belief
That a false-hearted promise is uglier than a thief
And you can tell it to Mr Brown sir yes go tell Mr Brown

We remember what you said sir before the troops were sent
"If you're not for us you're against us" so Mr President
You can take back Mr Brown sir you can have your Mr Brown

We know what you-all did sir to help us in our pain
You gave some cash to Halliburton and sent some ice to Maine
So we thank you very kindly sir we thank you Mr Brown

You can shoot me where I stand sir just to shut my gob
If you ever hear me say the words You've done a heckuva job
And we're mighty grateful to you yes we thank you Mr Brown

I'll tell you what I'd do sir if I had an enemy
I'd send Mr Brown and FEMA to give him help for free
Yes I'd send him Mr Brown sir I'd send in Mr Brown

We'll be bailing out our bedrooms and fighting starving rats
And fending off the cottonmouths and voting for Democrats
Who will thank you very kindly sir yes they'll thank you Mr Brown

Latin Roots

On Bourbon Street I bought two shirts I would never wear
in places where the air is cool and even.
I danced in doorways to tin beats
captured by soul and sweat.
My daughter was embarrassed by my transgressions
horrified by the foreign piece of me who drank beer
and loved strangers
giddy at the beggar with one leg
and the doo-wop boys in mismatched suits
strutting under curlicue canopies.
I stood on sidewalks ripe with the stench of excess and forgiveness
catching trinkets from tattered chariots
of masked men anonymous in their joy.
The concierge warned us,
"When you go out the front door, turn right, you'll be safe."
He showed us maps inscribed with icons
our routes predetermined
on the dexterous side.
The toothless black lady in the fancy four-star bathroom
rambled on about her ancestral home
on the sinister side.
"Oh yes'm, I'll never leave here.
I'll die in Great Great Gran-Daddy's house like my kin before me."
Did she suffer for the hoodoo gift of prophecy?
I gave her a dollar for her history
and a clean towel.
After the flood I learned new rhythms of truth.
The poor that died went to the left, while we found jambalaya.

Estha Weiner

New Orleans Has Collapsed!

In Appreciation of Frank O'Hara

I was watching the hurricane news
thinking it's bad but it's not as bad
as they thought when all of a sudden
it was worse   why??   the levees broke
and the water poured through the sexy sweet
City of New Orleans   through
cemeteries and jazz
Zydeco and oysters
booze and Blues
balconies and Brennan's
Black and White
Congregation Named Desire
Queen of the River Excess
did the God of those Righteous Boys
now running
the U.S. of A.
visit this flood upon your sensuous
banks   No   Noah in these Boys' plans
Oh New Orleans I love you get up !

Aftermath

A Street Called Humanity

After the hurricane rooftops, siding,
screen doors and windows drift to sea,
frightened policemen flee while the world watches
a man and a woman cling to their dog, two cats, to each other,
a father and son—waist high in water—wander streets,
push plastic containers filled with food, photographs, clothing,
a middle-aged woman in a boat floats alone
through floods of mud, wreckage and waste.

Helicopters alight, airlift lost children
aimless without siblings, mothers or fathers,
a young man won't leave his house,
a grandmother is dying and cannot be moved,
a woman weeps for her missing husband,
a mulberry tree rises through the debris,
a parakeet unable to fly sits on a broken window sill,
all of this, on a street called Humanity.

Thursday's refrain

Guy on the radio: we tie-off the dead ones.
Floaters.

After the hurricane, all houses are boat houses.
He's telling people to leave
or the army will drag them away.
What they hear: home home home home
stay.

Guy on the radio is crying.
I see my memory of a horse just then,
in the field across the river,
across the road across the trees,
across the sky across the day.
My mind floating on the idea of running away.

He says he doesn't remember any prayers.

Prayer of not sleeping for days.
Prayer of steering among the shoals of roofs.
Prayer of shaking the dead, just in case.

And the Lord said: let there be high ground, tree limbs,
cling unto the telephone poles,
cling.

I hear the guy on the radio looking up at the sky.
I hear the rope in his boat thinking of knots.
I hear sun drinking water away.

In my kitchen, these sounds from New Orleans
and a small breeze, a watchgear wind,
a follicle brushing of air,
wind the size of how it feels
to tie a dead girl to a porch rail,
rubs the microphone with gentle, good gentle breaths
of away.

Dear Latifah

I've been scanning this hell-hole
for your lost baby
terror in her clenched fists
mouth screaming desperation
lungs breathing stench
I've dragged myself past
toothless grandmothers
all of us flushed down
this putrid river of feces
water-logged cadavers
flowering with toxic mold

I am a woman of hate now
for the man in clean clothes
there is nothing here
that rhymes with hope.

The blue light of night strobes on granite
glare on the perfected grimace of our impostor
his tailored blue shirt-sleeves rolled up
as if he'd just come from sinking his hands
in fetid waters and infested earth
his mouth flat as if with sorrow
but he can not even imagine
the sound of your vicious grief
the way you inhale horror
and exhale the history
which will be told
no matter how long from now
how far from here

There are too many mothers
to swear your babies are dead
too many sisters witnessed your rape
too many walked the bridges

occupied by uniforms and deadly weapons
too many men gone holding up a glory flag
while not enough remained at home to set you free

I am a woman of hate now
for the man in clean clothes
there is nothing here
that rhymes with hope.

Chorus

One abandoned to water,
one fleeing from it.
In that wet fall of 2005,
the old did not take turns.

In New Orleans they set sail from their beds;
the women's long hair and pale gowns fanning out,
white pinwheels floating
on Lake Pontchartrain's runoff.

Outside Houston, a hulled and blackened bus
remembers them; their short pleasantries,
long silences, and how lightly
the elderly travel.

Did they feel cheated,
not so much by death itself, or its preventability,
but by each missing their solo;
their hushed time?

Or did they spin away with arms
linked, a slow vortex of unity,
synchronized swimmers who merged
in an epiphany of downed fences
after a lifetime of separate backyards?

And in that same day, a commune of distant souls
squeeze through together, then separate
into the slippery waters
of solitary birth.

Colleen J. McElroy

Basin Street

*"Armed Dolphins Let Loose
By Katrina"* The Observer, *September 2005*

half a block away from where the old men
used to hitch up their pants to do a soft shoe
shuffle the trees have turned grey with rot

on the corner where someone remembers a man
named Buck losing his mind back in '48
a car rests belly up in the muck wheels facing

the sky as if the Lord has summoned it to pray
and in the bayou less than twenty minutes away
levee gates lie frayed like seams on an old suit

if there was a warning nobody heard down
where the sea was held back by a few splinters
and hope—where sweet face dolphins gazed

longingly toward open waters before the storm—
and none were spared—not the dolphins trained
to kill—a fine kettle of fish the navy brewed—

not the poor who suffered bottom feeders
glutted on rubbish or a corpse: human dog
bird all the same loss of political clout

not the city washed over and over and out
to sea it all goes head over tail over
church over steeple and school

with no one to interrupt a Tuskegee
kind of bust away from where the buck
stops—the fecund wash of what's left

when you lose those Basin Street Blues
and somewhere at sea dolphins armed
to the teeth—unwilling soldiers/warrior

mules—cute if you ignore the knives
attached to flippers and snouts and wait
for what the water brings in/takes out

Elegy for the Hurricane Victim

Here they are safe, no ocean.
No choppy churned-up house flogging
gulf. No pock-marked, skeletal
levees breached, no home's
eroded copingstones.
No bones.

No,
they are the rescued ones, they embraced
the helicopter crewsmen, soared
into the sky. They rest in the powdery underbelly
of Houston's city lights. They have spilled
into the Inner Loop, clogged up the Astrodome,
flooded the roads. And yet they are here,
my mother not among them.

No, she said again, again, to friends
I sent to rescue her. *I know my son
will save me soon. No, really that's okay. No.*

I am three weeks late, yes,
but heading home at dusk, I find myself
easing onto the highway, unpacked
and rushing back east and skipping the
exit signs. I want to come back
and find her still praying, the door
standing open, her outstretched arms a broken
gutter collecting rainwater, drop by drop.

Dawn Evans Radford

A Peripheral Blow

For weeks after the storm,
the bay shrimper, fatigued
by tons of hurricane trash choking
his nets, and by meager gains of scarcely
succulent shrimp, would putter home
to throw himself upon the mercy of his
family church.

For weeks, the long-proud harvesters
of bay oysters, the oysterman
and his oyster shucker neighbor,
grieved in silence, waiting
while the estuary cleaned itself.

In a stoic and starving months-long wake,
they suffered through a further
catastrophe blowing its own ill winds:
distant, agenda-driven, myopic politics
that might some day bestow blessings,
grant them back their harvest rights
to the Gulf's pearl of produce,
its world-renowned bay of oysters.

Walter Bargen

Rescuers . . . pushed aside the dead

Let's see or not see, let's think or not think, but let's breathe because
we have no choice for the moment unless you're being dragged through
New Orleans in the petrochemical gumbo-gush of Lake Pontchartrain,
hearing a final time the gurgle of late night saxophones and the lapping
waves of applause as she teases off her pasties and thong in submerged
floodlights, crossing each new night's gulf of unbridgeable sadness, as
you spin past open doors smoky with water, above the sidewalk canopies
that cling to the sides of buildings like sunken canoes, and catch for a
moment a wrought iron lamppost with a limp arm, your whole body
limp, no longer face up to the sky, no longer face down, except to those
stranded on rooftops who see you pass as they wave their arms at passing
helicopters, the whump-whump-whump of defeat and rescue, as you
perform your trick, floating above the street, a slow-motion superman.
You didn't know that to gain superhuman powers you had to hold your
breath forever never to be rescued.

Alexis Spencer-Byers

Relief

September 18, 2005
Lutheran-Episcopal Disaster Response Center

Laid out on a flattened lawn chair
In the middle of a co-opted classroom
I attempt to sleep
But the stirrings and snores of a dozen other volunteers
Keep me awake and alert,
And punctuate the racing of my mind

We've come to this place to offer our aid
And I must believe that we've been useful
After many hours of screening, sorting, and sizing
Donated clothes—
Garments made noble by the bodies they will soon cover—
Sturdy folk who have survived this storm
With little more than their lives
And their ability to start over

And yet I think I must be beginning to know
How a drop of rain feels
When it lands in the ocean
Immediately overwhelmed by its smallness
And insignificance

Still, that drop is absorbed
And becomes part of a whole
Endowed with incomprehensible size and strength
By the God who brought each drop to that place and time
The same God whose Hand has summoned me here
To weed out winter jackets
Affix countless handmade labels
And scavenge for men's pants in a size 42

Gulf Bodies

Before their faces came in
and the water rose to the gulf
your twins were gone and you were glad

they didn't live to see. You stilled
with them, gathered up their coarse
blood left behind and pulled out.

(Women are told monstrous things
when their heels rest in the cool palms
of stirrups.) And you go

on rummaging through boxes for the one
thing that's worth saving: matchbooks
from Hotel Monteleone, a newspaper

clipping announcing a first engagement,
a pair of black steel binoculars
and their hard leather case (the leather

laces of the case's seams darker
than the rest of the leather).
Without names you know

they are gone forever into a black box,
an almost memory and unjustified.
Every day your breasts recede, back

to the shore of unmother. On the soft
blue light of the evening news, a real mother
has lost her real son in the storm. She cries,

looks through the glass at your belly
and cries, *I want my peoples. I want
my peoples. Don't have nobody else.*

Philip Overby

Please Don't Kill Me

I saw a house slumped over a tree, clinging to it like a baby koala,
its guts splayed out, tangled around the roots and limbs.
Five dishwashers, nine stoves, big white lice in clumps of dirt,
pulverized brick looks like crushed peppermints.

They emerge, attracted by the hum of machinery, the orange excavators
roaring and ripping into bark and broken mirrors.
The sign says "Danger, Asbestos Present" but they creep closer.

I'm a beacon to them, because I'm there to help
But I'm the governmental scapegoat, a cog in the slow wheels
of FEMA, FEMA they spit,
FEMA, they claw at my hands,
FEMA didn't give me this and that,
FEMA, the living machine,
all beating hearts and blood and wires and muck.
Their eyes insist that I make miracles.
I am the feral FEMA to them, the Elephant Man
trouncing the downtrodden, pulling up the skin of the innocent
with tusks of fire.

I am their Medusa head, they show me to FEMA and all is saved,
dream homes will sprout from the earth, shiny and new,
cracking away the shell of blackened, speckled ruin.
They dance and cackle rattling the bones of the workers,
meant to help and destined to fail.

I am here to observe only.
"Yes ma'am, yes sir, please don't kill me."
Everything is a conspiracy, everything a ploy.
The excavators line the horizon, their craning necks dip down,
their jaws plummet into nothingness, ripping into memories,
eating bras, lamps, bowls, sofas, muddy and slick.

The Woman on Mexico Street

My house is here,
roof like the Virgin's cloak
interior bright with the ghost
of bleach: a high, noiseless whine.

We're having hurricane spring: various skeletons
modeling honeysuckle. Dogwoods full length
on the ground, blooming their funeral.

The street owns more dogs
than people. The dogs and I don't recognize
each other. They run, dragging
invisible chains. I sit tight

with supplies of food
and thoughts that come back
like dogs. The bowl of dog food
empties by morning. The bowl of thoughts,
never. Like the shore,

I've taken early retirement.
We're all headed to the sea,
so why wait? Because, God knows,
the water is cold
and can't be trusted.

Salvage

She has to begin, she knows this,
but first she needs to think it through.
So she sits on the stoop and waits,
brushes a fly away from her face.
Her eyes close and her chin drops
to her chest like a stone,
as though whatever muscle and sinew
holding up her head has suddenly gone slack.
Elbows on her knees, she
rolls her head from side to side, and
from deep in her chest starts to hum
a song she hasn't thought of in years.

It's time to get started, time to do something,
she knows, she knows. But she is glued to the concrete step,
stunned like a fly smartly swatted but not killed.

She lights a Salem and puffs slowly,
absentmindedly picking at her cheek.
She sees a neighbor two doors down
loading a pickup with debris.
"When you're done over there
you can come over here," she mutters.

She looks up and down the street of what
was once a decent enough place to live.
She knows she needs to do something.

But it is getting onto late afternoon and the sun
is dropping below the taller rooftops. Maybe
she should just call it a day, go back to the motel
where her four kids and her cousin are waiting,
get everyone some supper.
"I got a start on it anyway," she will tell them.
"And tomorrow's another day."

Or maybe she should just start walking,
head west until her shoes wear down
to nothing, keep walking on the bare
soles of her feet, sanding them down
with each westward step, getting
shorter and shorter, she imagines,
until by the time she reaches the
Pacific Ocean, there is nothing left
but her head
to roll down the dunes into the surf.

John Cantey Knight

Silence Speaks Louder than a Poet's Words

In the aftermath of Katrina

Mary is a friend of mine. She has a
significant other, a really nice guy
who's Japanese-American and also a
craftsman. She and he restored a run-
down crack house to its 1824 glory:
pegged hand-sawed wood, cypress
shutters and flooring. Mary's garden
survived—the flooding in that part
of the 9th Ward wasn't so bad. "Lucky,"
I told her. Mary canes chairs when not
otherwise employed. By her first husband,
a former Vieux Carré Commission
Chairman, or president, she had a
daughter, who was, maybe is, a librarian.
Her house was elsewhere—Gentilly?
She stayed. Fifteen feet of water,
"Betsy" back in the Sixties proved
that it pays to keep an ax in the attic—
to hack through to the roof. Do you
remember the Superdome on TV?
She ended up there. "She was a talker,"
her mother said. "That was her nature.
How she could run on discussing
anything. Now, she won't say a thing,
not a word" about her descent into hell.
In Houston now, she's not coming back.

Broken Limbs

The broken half people opened like oysters, rummaged around a toothpick home, swollen antiques lay scattered in mud, poking out like fossils from a distant time, a marble, a dirty toothbrush standing tall, we pick like scavengers and find hope in a receipt, a matchbook. We scoop up the mud and get rid of debris, property lines crossing; a neighbors shoe rests comfortably on a broken limb. For an hour we tip the hard white shell of a Maytag back and forth, it sticks stubborn, but it finally gives way like our broken levee, we look down and stuck in the mud our family portrait, glass broken and faded too soon, it speaks to us in the open air, we hold it up to the light like pirates gold, walking along a sea of mud, we find pearls.

Marion Menna

Blue Monday

Antoine Domino, better known as Fats,
chose to stay at home for the hurricane.
Katrina, sweet little Dutch girl, blew
in at force five across the Gulf of Mexico.

He had survived one at five years of age,
some seventy years ago, believed
he could ride out the storm again,
but this wasn't Blueberry Hill.

One hundred and ten million records later,
Ain't it a Shame, who can blame him
for thinking himself a survivor—
but the 9th Ward of New Orleans

lies too low in the flood plain,
and the levees didn't hold up
under howling wind and rain,
wave surge and disrepair.

Checquoline Davis, his niece, posted
a message, pleading for information—
"last seen on the second floor
balcony—has anyone seen Fats?"

Our tears fell like rain and the moon
stood still. The four winds blew
'til blue Monday when Fats came
walking, yes indeed, still walking,
out of the dome.

Miss Mary

In a voice that carries across the room
the white-haired woman talks to volunteers
who dish out chili, beans, crackers, and fruit.
God bless you all, she says, *I'm a poet, you know.*
I'll write a poem about this later.

She wanders the aisles between tables, then sidles
next to a young Hispanic woman with five stair-step girls
and little English. The mother settles her children,
a polite smile on her lips. *I was born in Canada, you know,*
but left as a baby. I'm part English but I belong here now.

"Here" is a shelter filled with Hurricane Rita evacuees
who have driven or bussed in from the Gulf Coast.
Their towns are closed, their homes destroyed or damaged.
No light, no water, belongings left behind for flood waters,
rain, high winds. *I was in the army in Florida, driving people*
around. Once Eleanor Roosevelt came and I drove her too.

The white-haired woman is thin, has pale skin, is old;
her clothes from Goodwill, her manners from better days.
All she has left is her voice and her stories. Once in a while
she wears a paper pinned to her blouse that says, "I can't talk."
She laughs. *Sometimes the Lord tells me to shut up and I do.*

The volunteers wonder about her history, her mental state,
where she comes from. The eyes of her neighbors glaze
over. They nod, fill themselves with food prepared
by Baptist men in yellow hats who came ready to fix 10,000
meals a day, are disappointed we only need 4,000.
Every night the woman says, *Give my regards to the chef.*

She blesses us as she picks up her food, reading our tags
and calling us by name; we don't know hers, are afraid to ask
because she will stop, interrupt the smooth flow of paper plates

from one carboy to another. We overhear her say *I'm Mary Smith*.
We like the anonymity of the name; it's as nebulous as her stories.
I'm an author, you know, and I'll write about you all some day.

Her blouse is a vee-neck of cream polyester with purple violets,
her cotton knit pants dark blue; she wears green footies, no shoes.
But her back is straight and she glides through the line, pausing to study
each pan of food as if she's at an elegant buffet, not a gymnasium,
or perhaps she does think it's a restaurant, for each table holds bouquets
of fake flowers in colorful plastic pots.

Are the television people here? They called me, wanted to talk with me,
interview me really. I don't mind it. I can tell them a lot. Our heads shake
but she doesn't seem disappointed, just studies the vanilla pudding
we have scooped from foot high cans into a deep aluminum tray.
She pats the hand of a volunteer who brings her a Styrofoam cup
of sweet iced tea. *You'll go far, my dear.*

The morning she misses breakfast, we fret among ourselves until
we hear her voice at the coffee urn telling strangers a tale of growing
up in England. But last night, she grew up in Louisiana, so what to believe?
We just wonder where she is going after the shelter closes, she is so alone.
My husband's relatives don't like me. They tell me to go to a doctor.
I went to five doctors but they refused to see me.

She gazes in the mirrored wall behind us, fluffs her white hair, winks at
    the girl
offering Oreos, Nutterbutters, Lorna Doones. *You're very important, you*
    know.
God bless what you're doing. But by week's end her façade is crumbling;
she is catching a cold. She can't keep track of whether she should talk or
    not.

She sits alone, eats little, watches the number of evacuees dwindle, hears of
a move to another shelter. The Red Cross worker helps her complete a
    form.
I was born in 1912. I don't know where I'll go from here.

Daniel Crocker

Government Cheese

for Sherman Alexie

I, too, was poor
and ate government cheese
and squirrel
and other things
people forget
what a trailer park really is
a ghetto
bathtub meth
your cousin
coming down with *it*
the hook
the kind of place
it's hard to write
yourself out of
the taste
of government cheese

The place of broken down Buicks

A place the wind can pick up
on a whim called Katrina
and wipe clean
and ain't nobody
gives a damn.

The Storm Seduction

Reckless and fickle to the end,
    the storm
moves on with a last cold shrug
    of the sky,
leaving behind the hysterical flashes
    of trucks and squad cars,
rivers of mud lashing
    placid suburban lawns,
fractured oaks crucified on their own trunks
    but never to be resurrected,
the ghosts of blind traffic lights
    hovering over dead, directionless ponds,
lines of leaderless cars looking
    for a place to turn around,
for a street the storm neglected
    to seduce and abandon,
for a road that knows
    the way home,
if there's still a home whose ravished walls
    have not bled to death.

Gina Ferrara

While Water Touched the Eaves

—December 27, 2005

My mother's house turned upside down,
the last few grains in an hourglass,
pink insulation avalanched from the ceiling
and fell in blinding clouds and tufts to the floor
while water touched the eaves.

The house plummeted through dream sequences
and nightmares, the rapid eye movement of shutters,
doors and windows unhinged in the course of one night
rooms shifted time zones, tottering on the slab,
while water touched the eaves.

A flounder with vertebrae poking through scales
swam in the saltwater deluge, through my mother's house
for refuge on the verge of extinction
with all those family mementos
remains of fish and photos affixed to the brick
while water touched the eaves.

Philip C. Kolin

FEMA Cities

They're building
FEMA cities for
Temporary people
Humanity on its way
Into weeks, months, years
Of trailer captivity.

But their estranged uncle-landlord
Doesn't want them
To get too cozy
So he's taking out
Unnecessary necessities
Like insulation
From a fretful future
Or house numbers
That say they belong
Somewhere other than today.

Instead of having foundations or piers
These G.I. cells are propped on corroding rubber wheels.
If they sink
Into post-Katrina terra infirma
They are subject to be being towed to oblivion.

Then Bill Clinton will be right:
They will have no place
To go to
And no way
To get there.

After the Flood

1.
It's true. On the Greater New Orleans Bridge,
the Gretna police fired over the heads

of those fleeing the flood. Don't ask
what I would have done. There's comfort

in distance, comfort in saying: "If it happens
again, I'll do the same damn thing."

The police chief means he's not sorry?
Or he knows, either way, he's damned?

2.
As ordered, the Marines in Al Hayy shot up
the car that kept roaring toward the roadblock

after the warning shots. The Marine who searched
the car for weapons and explosives, he's the one

who should be telling you this. The two men
who stumbled out of the car unharmed. Unarmed.

The three-year-old girl curled in the back seat.
The top of her skull, when the Marine picked her up,

sliding open, this story spilling out. Please don't
ask what I would have done. There's no comfort

in hearing the father say, "I'm sorry." No comfort
hearing the Marine who clutched the girl, confess,

"This is the event that's going to get me
when I go home."

3.
In the backyard, where it's still jungle, I find
a shotgun shell. Whose blood spilled here?

I drop the shell into my pocket. Evidence
for a court that will never meet. By the chainlink fence,

a dusty pumpkin slumbers through September.
Next spring, vines will grow here once again, thick

and stubborn. What will I do? With gloves
and hatchet, I'll disappear into the tangle.

Katrina Watch

What can one say of
utter devastation?

*You should have listened
to us beforehand.*

*You should have gotten out
of the way.*

*What you had was not
worth preserving.*

*Clearly God was punishing
your wickedness.*

*You're better off starting anew
in a strange place.*

Dry voices ringing
like cracked church-bells

except the one true
tolling:

I am sorry. I will help.

Who knows what sun feels
scorching the Sahara, swallowing
caravans of the faithful,

lava raging over mountains
with huts and villagers
like potage?

Waters taking aim
from their deadly gun-wales.

Nature does not speak
its cruelty.

Yet rebirth begins:
seeds of lodgepole pine sprouting
after fearsome fires, green

saplings only days
after black, black death.

We who speak
can articulate sympathy,
assistance, rebirth.

The hours of hammering.

Witness like owls who have taken
up a collection of eyes,

perch in
the nearest eaves

calling for our neighbors.

Steve Dalachinsky

invisible ray # 28

—labor day weekend

6 spots
then 3 &
out
i think he meant 5 or
10 (imagination(is

    summer
scaffolding itself around
  the coming fall

it's the first 3 day holiday
that i'm not glad to be having off

donald is already stacking firewood
in his head
to verify a life
still lived
his hands
lung
a labor of patience
his birthday soon to be behind him
again
barbecued

later the small reddening puffs
of clouds will slowly make their way
across the sky between bldings
where the music will drench my hot tired
self as ". . . pity divides the soul
                    and man unmans."
as sorrow for others is drowned
deep within my heavily lined pockets

this weekend
i will collect part of the money
owed me

buy a set of colored pencils
& a 50 cent belt
off the street
its memories
will immediately sift thru my nostril
like all the quinine ever used to cut dope

tonight i will dream
that i am being hoisted upward
away from polluted water
death
flowers
friends
government
rats
rabbits
prisons &
pigs

no more dirty laundry for a while
poisoned glass gloves
my feet dangling safely above
the filth

in the dream i will be frightened by
a "Negro"
but this is a good sign & one that denotes
safety

when i wake
i will paint onions on my garlic
snapshot the damn picture for
posterity
(fed the same images over & over again)
kiss Precious Slaughter good morning
rescue the bacon
ignore the gallows & the
hearse
& armchair the good weather
& the birds.

Duane Morrison

Far from the Big Muddy

Starlit maniacs grope
amid angel stricken flesh.
Vanished comforts and fear
the new beast to tame.

With drained mantles of strength,
time is enemy and savior.
Shallow loss comes early
in Job-like waves of sea.

Maggot dogs are neighbors now.
Strangers adrift with command in tow;
guns and butter at hand,
singing 'bread of life' for a price.

Stranded in the bosom of hell,
choices linger like boils.
Hidden killers of lassitude;
resent squats in regret's house.

Stories harvest relief as
desert cubes distract downpours
far from the big muddy bowl
that gave hope a new game.

Kenneth Pobo

When I Saw

the faces of those stranded
in New Orleans,
mostly black, mostly poor,
I remembered sitting in
the Café Du Monde

the previous May sipping
chicory coffee, eating
three beignets, and how glad
I was to be getting over a cold
among flowers and music,

later to walk the same streets
that Irma Thomas, the soul queen
of New Orleans, walks—Bush's
face appeared suddenly, his
smug grin, his mom saying

poor people are used
to refugee camps—I pictured
him and his family wandering
in muck for days,
no water, no food,

no news about who is alive
and who isn't,
water from a busted levee
rushing toward them,
nothing to stop it.

Walter R. Holland

The Yellow School Buses

Yellow as flowers in a field, the un-driven buses
sat, loaves of an uneaten bread. Instructive really
they hold the memories of simple arithmetic, addition
and subtraction—history lessons. What students
do they wait for? The test is over, that jeering team
has lost the game. No riders here, no diligent children
with hands in their laps, just the dazed faces
waiting for the long road home.

Pretend

Pretend you don't know me and I can't walk
and you lift me up and carry me everywhere.
Pretend I'm so hungry I don't remember how to swallow.
All week, I've been turning off the television
every time it shows pictures of families on rooftops
children floating away. I don't have to explain
to my granddaughter what it's like to have no home.
Long before the President got ready
for what he kept calling a "really big storm,"
Josie was practicing being evacuated.
I suspect that at five she has a better idea
of what it'd be like to lose everything
than a man who went to Yale and made his fortune in oil.
Who knows better than a pre-schooler
what it's like not to be able to control your fate?
She's not too young to learn
how to beg. Today we went up to people on the street
and Josie held out her jar in front of strangers
as if she could see in them a goodness they don't even suspect.
She stood there till it was obvious her arm was aching.
We made several hundred dollars.
Not a bad day's work for a five-year-old and her grandfather.
Josie and I sat at the kitchen table
and counted money. What better way to learn addition?
It's a world of disturbing coincidences
and so you try everything you can
to make it seem as if there is no tragedy
you can't do something about.
And then it was time to play again.
If you're five years old, you can tolerate the real world
for only so long. *Pretend you open the door and there's a child*
in the bitter cold. She's got nothing to eat.
And so I sweep her off to the sofa,
cover her with three blankets and the cat
and feed both of them toast and milk

till Josie tires of getting well and is back at the door
feverish and knocking. Over and over she's orphaned
and lost and sick. *Pretend the other children have been rescued.*
But not me. Then you hear something.
You think it's just the wind at first.
Maybe you have to lift a whole tree off me.
Pretend you think that I'm dead
and you go to bury me and I open my mouth
but I can't make a sound come out of me.
I look like a just-born bird.
Pretend I am a bird fallen from a tree
and so you have to teach me how to fly.

Jim Elledge

Mister Betwixt and Between

After a few days, Mister doesn't watch
the news: too much human despair: famine,
disease, war, and the eye that never blinks:
not "the tube"—well, *that*—but the hurricane
that sucked up and spat out the Big Easy,
its swirl God's fingerprint—or Satan's.
Mister wonders, stirring his martini,
With human misery, what's the difference?
Taking sips, his thoughts drift to Frankenstein. . . .
(He can't help how like a madcap séance
his mind's become, a big top of slapstick.)
He channel surfs a sec—sitcoms, reruns,
cop schlock, infomercials, soaps, and cartoons—
and picks a reality show to watch.

Washboard

Take the corrugated tin and backward bayou spoon.
Take the stage.
Accept the rhythm like a buried child.

The all-night vivifiers show
hands-on-hips surprise
that you remember basic parts
you've amputated to survive
somewhere else in the world.

In this Rue Dauphine juke joint
you cut off conversation
with the croak strafe
of an instrument made for purgatory.

The city would be at your feet
if it hadn't just scattered
now that you've finally returned.

Any Cajun, any Zydeco band
on Rue Bourbon or Rue Royale
will take you. You're the one
with the fewest beers
and what passes for the beat.

Chances are you're white,
but if your pockets jangle
it doesn't matter, it never did,
except to you,
here in America's drain guard
where anyone could kiss you on the mouth,
and your crude technique reminds us
music has no name.

When the water came,
no one missed you but the city,
whose dark streets on an endless night
you would swear are breathing,
because it's the music
made from drudgery's tools
that keep it alive.

The beignet waitress,
all powdered sugar,
catches melody in her frosty hair
and sings it to the weary river.

She and the city follow you home,
like friendly, mangy dogs
who sit by your stereo,
digging the Dixieland brass.

The city has every face
that bobs by the bar,
all the chests and hands
that hold and scratch tin furrows,
the eyes that plead for peace
in our country, in our time,
too aware our time,
like the washboard's,
requires depthless art
to keep its tuneful why
inside a meager head.

Something Big and Aloud Is Coming
To Blow All My Burdens Away

> *"Be Prepared"*
> *—The Boy Scout Motto*

I.   During the Wet Season

> *"Torn by dreams,*
>
> *By the terrible incantations of defeats*
> *And by the fear that defeats and dreams are one."*
> —Wallace Stevens

There were children to be neglected,
muddy shoes which left no tracks.

All was solemn and so-so
very misunderstood.

Everything was owing to God's grace,
His celestial umbrella. For He

        who ruled the earth and waves
        there were no rain delays.

           There were oaths
           to be broken.

I stood in the batter's box,
mine eyes hone like puddles

(shards of glass, left over
from the incidents).

Ruin ran in runnels, the ditches—slick
with disaster.

There were women.
There was a woman
—all dried up and blown away.

Above all a desert boomed,
abloom with lies and blasphemies.
Crowds roared.

II.   The Ventriloquist's Voicebox,
      The Dummy's Aside

Here is but another version
of myself.   *How?* you ask.
Why? I reply.

Gather together these stones,
these twigs, this dust. Fill your mouth.
Then,
call them by their names: *my guides, my runes,*

my eyes. Better still:
My Lost and Found. Dig down.
Deep. Deeper.   Deeper, still—

            past Vaudeville,
            past Hollywood,
            past Mommy and Daddy.

Come closer, examine the earth
from which life debarks—into which
life recedes. *What have you found?*

Some clues: *paraclete,*
purblind, paean, padrone.
And more: *ascete, cryptic,*

eliminate. A question: *What have you*
lost?
Everything.

Where? you ask.
Now,
It replies.

III. The Drowning

Eat My Bread (*this is My Body*) and drinketh
from My cup (*this is My Blood*) which runneth over,
sayeth The Lord, God Almighty—resplendent
in a silk smoking jacket,

fine raiment for a gentleman of means, of
meaning.

At Center Stage: an ash
drops
from His cigarette, ominously,
into a cup of swirling
coffee . . .

The people tried to be good but could not.
In New Babylon, the rain poured down in shrouds.
You ask: *Why? Why does a good and loving God*

permit such calamity, especially, to the least of his fold?
And still:
the rains come, mixed with the sea

and the fishes and the serpents—and the woebegone
cling helplessly to the eaves
and rooftops crying, *Mercy!*

Why?   For this reason:
Lo! when we were asked the most fated
question asked in all of time—we rose

and roared in unison: *Give us Barabbas!*
So what means this? rape,
pillage, thirst, famine,

pestilence, the indifference of the sovereign?
Forsooth: life is naught
save for truth—and *consequence*.

New Orleans

In the city of masks,
You seek the tangible, the real,
Like the homeless man asleep,
His cheek against the church wall,
A child nestling his mother.
You flee the tarot cards,
Seeking sanctuary where icons are touched.
You kneel before Mary Madonna
In the alabaster cathedral,
You want to trust her,
Her mirror never betraying
The changes in your face.
In the end you turn away,
As the steamboat whistles through the open door.
Instead, you invoke the name of Marie Leveau,
Love for the price of gris-gris,
Take your chances with Saint Expedite,
His name on a wooden crate.
He takes you to a bar on Bourbon Street,
Where you see the priest and the pimp
Throwing for snake eyes,
All spun out on the wheel of fortune.

You run out of the bar,
Into the city streets,
Alone, always alone,
Your heart up in your throat,
Searching for John Dilman.
He held out for Ophelia
When the rest of the police force
Had closed the book on her,
Written her off as a simple hit and run.
It's his blessing you seek,
As you ride the streetcar,
The warm, tropical air hitting your face,

As you escape to Elysian Fields,
In an upstairs room in
A house in the Garden District
At the end of the line.

TV images in your room
Of that perfect spiral,
A thing of beauty, you thought,
How Nature repeats patterns in
Galaxies, seashells, the cochlea of the ear.
That deadly roulette wheel of fate again,
Spinning, spinning over the dark water.
Everyone in church, praying it away
From the city of Saint Joan.
But you saw in your mind the cards
All falling to the floor.
Wash all my sins away, you said,
As the flood waters rose.
Let me drown in the tears of
These lost children,
These abandoned animals.
The waters rising into your throat,
Falling down your checks.

You always knew that Jesus would come back,
Rowing a tiny boat.
Instead, it's an angel with muddy boots,
Who picks up your ragged skirts from the floor
And gathers your medicine.
Quietly you take his arm, your head held high.
"Au Revoir," I will return, you thought,
Maybe open a little hat shop
On Rue Royale, just as Tennessee Williams
Used to say Blanche would do.
Whispering softy, "La Nouvelle Orleans toujours."
Hearing cathedral bells in the courtyard
You pass the garden gate,
Still standing beside the sweet olive,
Still blossoming with gardenias
Still promising the camellias.

Katrina Tankas

I

Grass lives (even thrives)
Amidst the devastation
Shocked into greenness
We're all leading public lives
Tending our inner gardens

II

Who is left to pray?
Gaia has her language too
An eerie medley
The sea's disembodied voice
A sorrow without a name

III

The feel of damp grass
A finger that does not move
No liquor to dull the ache
Of this wordless narrative
Of loose bricks and empty hats

IV

The graffitied wall
In a heap as if shot up
Like your friend's husband
Doing who-knows-what downtown
Murder most foul

V

Open the garage
Slowly and manually
Come face to face with the truth:
Pines do not always stand tall
Acting is a fearful choice

VI

Who has drawn our lives?
Random clouds assume a mask
Nasty surprise looms
The old dealer vends bad cards
Molten silver streaks the sky

VII

Morning thunderstorms
The air steeped in petrichor
Awake and rejoice
Tree limbs scattered everywhere
We two are alive alive

Jerry W. Ward

Warning from La Papessa to the Tourists

If you are
In New Orleans
Before, during, after
Mardi Gras

And see people
In the streets weeping
Oily green tears

Do not touch them
Or speak to them
They are Katrina's children

They are the virgins
Of the city
Repossessed by stigmata

Stigmata are contagious

Rescue

"Everyone is shining their flashlights, so as you're flying over,
it's kind of like you see a sky full of sparkling stars.
So which star do you pick?"
— Helicopter pilot, after Hurricane Katrina

It's no more random than anything else in life.
Think of all those lights shining in the dark—
the children of famine holding up their empty bowls,
the battle wounded waiting for a medic,
the homeless milling outside the overcrowded shelter,
the hapless victims held at gunpoint,
the sick lying on their pallets at Bethesda,
the dying trapped by fire, flood, earthquake, avalanche,
the living.

Rescue, if it comes, is only temporary.
The pilots, medics, aid workers, police—
so few, so fallible.
But high above them the Creator of Light
patrols the dark, counting the stars.
None are missed, all accounted for.

Mama's Gardenias

—for Metairie, Louisiana

Born at Charity, where my father interned,
I learned snakes and hurricanes in Metairie,
Our homeplace, a house graced with gardenia bushes
Like a necklace of pearls. My childhood hurricanes
Came and went, like snakes in the backyard—
All poisonous deadly, until Dad says they're not.
We knew what to do

With flashlights and flooding, vaccinations
And radios. The canal at the end
Of our Green Acres Road slid sly
Into our living room, up to the piano
Poised on bricks, while we rode
The boats of our beds all night,
Watching the hurricane's dark blood
Soak into our carpet. The wind bansheed
Through our front door's edges, a scream
Like that of a grass blade blown
Between the space in two paralleled thumbs.

After, we'd lower the green rowboat
From the carport beams, row to the corner market
For bread and news. Mama shoveled mud
From under the piano, trimmed ragged gardenias.
When the canal coaxed water away,
We'd ride bikes through the puddles and sludge,
Put bare feet up on the handlebars when
We saw a snake.
                    We knew what to do.

In Missouri, I heard Katrina scream
Through the TV as she tore into the coast.
She shoved the ocean so far upland
That levees broke we knew for years

Could break, and people were trapped
Who the world knew were left behind, waiting
Too many days for the kindness of strangers.
Charity melted into a house of horrors.
Metairie's gardenias blackened and rotted.

New species of snakes uncoiled—named
Elapse obsoleta resculum, Serpens viridis politicus,
And a Texas-morphed *Verbalis contortrix horridus.*
How can the people know what to do
When snakes walk upright, eat cake,
And buy shoes far from the drowning fields?

Mourning

Stella Nesanovich

The Sinking of New Orleans

This is the doomsday manual for the city you love:
antique buildings where you schooled, lush green
landscapes, and Canal Street where you shopped,
bearing pedestrians in thigh-high water.

Bienville's town, doomed since its founding,
a delta with houses like hyacinths perched
on verdant petals, a city forever needing
prayers to St. Jude, divine intercession.

Dryades, street of forest nymphs, neighborhoods
honoring the Muses, Marigny and Bywater:
sunk and watered. A thousand dead at least,
unable to escape on clotted roads.

Some stayed for pets or precious mementos,
Aunt Bessie's pearls, photographs warped
by rain before the lake shatters levee walls,
bones of ancestors float from graves.

(Futile your plans for ashes interred with theirs.)
Raised cottages in the Ninth Ward cannot
resist the steady seeping; the old streets
curl about the river, the lake,

like a friend's betraying tongue licking
the sides of houses, chewing off paint,
gnawing the cedar beams of old estates,
for hurricanes do not respect place,

do not swerve for history's sake,
follow relentlessly the old slave routes.

After the Waters

how do you grieve
the loss of a life
when it's yours
and you're still
alive and news reports
count you as dead
or near dead a refugee
in your own house
or what's left of it

how does death
become a statistic
when bodies bubble
up from loose branches
of streets turned
sour with the muck
of a system gone bad
homeless and heartless
in one fell swoop

and when the waters
recede how can you say
where you are when
maps are submerged
atop smudged roofs
and your bedroom
window tilts at some
odd angle sending
your family's history
to inconsolable depths
below the water line

where do you go when
all you've got is doomsday
profiteers and you've run out

of mother wit and the fabled
city you once lived in
has vanished like some double
page spread in *National
Geographic* its secrets exposed
for centuries to come

Stella Nesanovich

Five Miles South of Abbeville

A friend put his boat in the water
right in the middle of Highway 330,
seeking his grandmother's house
in Henry, where a dead cow floated
to the ceiling, the tide rising through
Vermilion into the homes of many a Cajun,
unearthing the dead of Erath and Port Sulphur.

He would rescue the stranded, people
and pets, his grandmother's china
and pictures, warped and moldy.
In the home of my cousins in Chalmette,
water and oil coat the land,
destruction dictating the path
of a freezer straight to the front.

I fled north, to a small church where
I sheltered for weeks, find I am blessed:
a tree ruptures only one room of my home
and I have time to contemplate the losses
of a girlhood friend in New Orleans East,
a poet and his wife whose lifetime
work vanished. The pink stucco houses

of Gentilly are scarred with sludge,
and the churches are under six feet of water,
the churches where I once prayed
funeral masses for my sisters.
An unholy baptism for my parents'
tombs among the raised cottages etched
with debris. Nephews and nieces

have fled to Arkansas and Tennessee
while I carry heart-breaking grief
into the new year. We are all undone—

my friend who put his boat in the water,
found animals floating amid the crystal
and china, the warped photographs,
the relics of shattered lives.

Gina M. Streaty

The Fourth Rose of Sharon

For Mother Ethel Mayo Freeman and Herbert Freeman, Jr.

What blooms in St. James Parish?
Ninety-one years
near the Third Rose of Sharon.

When the she-beast left,
so did you, swallowing
final breaths in liquid heat
outside a convention center.
For how many days?

Did you protest silently?
A ghost for the living,
a faceless number
slumped in a wheelchair;
a soiled, pouched blanket
to haunt evening news. . .

He said you often walked
from your door to church,
before you bore feeding tubes,
a pacemaker; before the back
of Louisiana was whipped raw.

He said he *wanted to stay* with you,
to plant himself beside you,
the lone withered bloom
on Jordan's banks.

Instead, he cradled you
too late and too soon
in a flawless casket—
the hue of you,
Rose.

Requiem for Amandine

My favorite restaurant drowned.
The one where for seventeen years
I ate dinner on Saturdays.
The bartender poured a Black Russian
as soon as I walked in the door.
The seafood gumbo was dark and rich,
with bits of turtle and turtle eggs,
and I kept pouring in the sherry
until it was almost a drink.
They made the best undressed shrimp loaf
for miles around,
but above all they made trout amandine,
crisp and floating in butter.
What's Saturday night to me now?

J'ai passé devant ta porte
says the old Cajun song:
I passed by your door, but you were not there.
The water mark is up to my eyes.
The bar is torn out—that brass rail was there
since the speakeasy days.
I found a plate of dishes on the sidewalk
and took one:
my first and only theft.
It helps me remember.

Come back, my city, my love,
return from the mud.
Let the dead refrigerators
bury their dead.
Pour a Black Russian, my beauty.
Bring me my favorite restaurant,
my Saturday sacrament,
my miracle of loaves and fishes.

Jazz Memorial

for R. P.

While the band jams,
      your widow passes out
beads as bright as grief.
    I tap my feet
          to "When the Saints . . ."
             and count blessings
     drowned and decayed
               even here, a year after.
You wanted a celebration,
        but I'm stuck in this mud
of memory with my voice
     too moldy to shiver
         to the beat
            of what you didn't believe
    though everyone else is singing
              your syncopated Orleans,
      raising up the dead,
this city's misery out on the streets
           unable to miss a parade.

Ella Singer

Vieux Carré

The last time I walked around her
        She was a fading rose
Clenched between mulatto secrets,

Her Creole charm threadbare,
        A moth eaten shawl
Wrapped around alabaster promises.

She was once shameless,
        The belle of many balls,
Breaking the rules of Dixie,

One hardly recognizes the lady now,
        Antebellum Delta Queen,
Sinking to her knees.

The Vieux Carré washed from her memory,
        Her mansions abandoned, but
Her people bound to the land by rituals.

Once the beauty mark on the face of the south,
        She was mistress to Spain, Africa, and France,
All conspired to secure her purchase.

Nola, when will I walk around you again?
        Pray in your cathedral?
I will remember the Ramparts, the carnival, the wild

Magnolia Indians, watch from the citadel so that
        I may speak of them once more
To the next generations.

Resolutions

John Kinsella

Canto of Rebuilding

A strong easterly blows through ghostly
radishes: dried brittle, seed-pod-spires,
menoras in vast profusion, the unliving shell

encasing the deeply sleeping, the waiting.
Mail isn't delivered this far out of town,
though trash is emptied, wheeled

forever down gravel roads, a low rumble
like a train fully loaded with grain—it takes
months to move it to the coast, out to sea.

Months have passed since the hurricane
tore New Orleans apart, a couple of weeks
᾿since a cyclone ripped up northern Queensland.

Last week, a Category 5 hit the Pilbara coast.
The winds picked up in Purgatorio,
the earthly paradise trembled and no one

ventured up there. Out back, John has been
breaking up the airframe of an old Cessna—
cutting through with hacksaw and welder,

shearing rivets which litter the ground
like eyes of seagulls peering up into the sun,
unblinking, out of their demography.

He took it platonically to the scrap-metal yard
this afternoon; the place depleted,
faint echo of depletions elsewhere

that melted down are recast, and rebuilt.
In some places they recycle cities, they'd learn
from mistakes, they'd list the lost on memorials.

Our three-year-old, citizen of many places,
tells us he is ordering his dreams for the night.
For him, sleep is building, rebuilding.

At sunset, the rivets shift focus, seagulls
flown back to the coast, small night birds
awakening, an implosive silver glint

as the last rays are broken, leaps
into the haze of memory: in Louisiana,
just after Katrina, I heard families

moving for shelter in anger, despair,
alone-ness, isolation, dismay, frustration—
nothing could be rebuilt in the same way.

I have been distressed by the unfathomable
death of a wattle tree, ground cracking
at the heart of an ant colony—

movement subterranean, even more
so than air, oceans: sweeping emergence,
seed-pods split with the barometer;

the weight of a mouse crossing
a roof beam, bark clinging to a fence-rail,
a rivet missed in the clean-up—

these too are to be given: commonplace,
                    if secretive.

Puzzle

We folk must go back
to the city we evacuated
though we do not know what to expect
at the military checkpoint
under the eye of the sun
and we do not have to try on courage
as if it were a pair of alligator boots
because we could touch stars
because we could spew copper
because we could fling light

We folk must not turn our backs
on the Creole city we call home
though we do not know the shape
we will take at finding our houses
just blown apart and soaked
and we do not have to ask anyone
to pick up the rough fragments
of our lives strewn everywhere
a brittle puzzle
between the dark and dank silence.

After Katrina: The Bodies Are Rising

Unjust death can never be
          contained in a crypt.

Bodies rising tend to expose
          the truth about the remains
          of Jim Crow days.

Atrocities are historic in Louisiana.
          Ghosts of old Creoles
          are again trying to speak:
"Where have y'all been?"
"Why did y'all leave us?"

          We are witnessing the
          sins of the last century
as mulattoes, quadroons, and octoroons rise.
Anti-Civil Rights Dixiecrats
          never wanted anyone to
          bother with the horrors
that *lie* just under the surface.
How many times will America allow
          the ugly issue of skin color
          to hemorrhage in our hearts.

New Orleans, you've always been a
          showy and Jazz mad city.
                    Please "Satchmo" come back
                    and jam with Wynton Marsalis—
                    blow the life back from
          smithereens to New Orleans.
"Oh, Susanna . . . don't you cry for me"
          and don't ever forget Emmett Till
          beaten so savagely his momma
          didn't know him.

"I'm going to Louisiana"
>not you, Dred Scott, unless you go back
>as a slave because the 1857 Supreme
>Court decision sealed your fate.
"With my banjo on my knee."
>It's time America,
>the bodies are rising.

How to Host a Hurricane:
Gov Love, American Style

Locate your home and loved ones
Far north of Danger. Label everything
South as "SEP." This increases
Your flippancy potential.

Bury your obvious faults in a levee.
You've graduated:
Forget history and physics.

Deliver a Brown Horse Head
To save the Coast, and please
Include his chef; the menu
Was insufferable.

Buy buses with wheels that go
'Round and 'round,
if they had drivers.

Marvel with your friends
That people without cars
Didn't drive out of danger.

Feign shock to hear
New Orleans called "Chocolate."
Forget that you stirred the meltdown.

Proclaim rebuilding will take
Ten years, as if we all
Can go cryogenic until then.

Ignore that this was a land
Of, by, and for the people
Who dreamed their government
Would be the same.

Diane Elayne Dees

Things To Do While You Wait for the Roofer

Try to find your friends.
They are probably tied up in traffic
somewhere in Texas and will be back
soon, except for those who will
never get off the highway.
You remember the last time you stood
in their houses; you picture the antique tables,
the blue Scandinavian dishes, the rose-colored depression
glasses, the shelves of books and photographs.
They are all waterlogged, smashed, reeking of mold,
or gracing the halls of looters. Your friends do not want
to talk to you, anyway. They have talked enough—
to adjusters, landlords, tenants, attorneys, bureaucrats.

Find a stump grinder. Hire a brick mason. Do something
about the ripped-off gutter. Put the mailbox on a log
so the cable company can knock it off again.
Leave home an hour early because the traffic is so bad.
Throw the dead plants away. Wonder where the owl went.
Adjust to the bare patches in your yard. Wait weeks for packages
to arrive. Feel guilty because you lost some trees and some
time and your roof is wrecked, but your friends are in Texas
and people you do not know are in trailers if they are really, really lucky.
Feel guilty because you complain while others have no jobs
or cannot find their beloved dogs and cats or their dead mothers.

Drive to New Orleans and marvel at how easily
you can find a parking place now. Momentarily forget yourself
and try to visit your old haunts. Count the refrigerators
on each block. Go to Lakeview and see the empty houses,
the cars left in parking lots, tossed together—giant playing pieces
on a board game. Banks, restaurants, coffee shops, schools,
churches, gas stations, grocery stores, pharmacies, gift shops—
all dark, abandoned, boarded. A couple in gas masks inspect
a house. The park is brown brush, the roses and red trains gone,

the carousel horses all dressed up with no place to go.
Keep your mouth closed if you can.

Pour yourself a drink and watch the news.
Get a grip on your rage.

Julie Morrison

Sweet as King Cake

Easy for you to say
Why don't I just move?
Because I'm rooted
Like a Banyan tree
In generations of cousins,
South's old 90/30
Everything I learned is here.
Everyone I know is here.
Everywhere I went was here.
All I've ever breathed
Was this tropical air
Sweet as King Cake
Warm as crème brûlée
Sunshine hot as red pepper
Traditions bind, family ties that
Don't blow away like daily news
Or wash away like gypsy dust.

Jerry W. Ward

After the Hurricanes

for the radical writers of New Orleans

Poverty is not devoid of its dignity
Nor is the Ninth Ward a fractured mirror
For minor gods to behold factitious laughter.
Beware of aliens, of inside agitators, of vultures
Who would batten on grief and broken hearts,
Kidnap our cultures and dreams, dreams wondrously aged
Transport and auction them for abuse.
Against such tragedy within tragedy we stand
In solidarity for life, for liberty, for return to happiness.

Hope is not devoid of its deceit
Nor immune to misleading into swamps.
Careful. Don't move left. Quicksand be there.
Don't move right. Gators will kiss you.
Learn from the fugitives enslaved.
Befriend moccasins.
Capture and coffle the cruel,
The arrogant, the mammon cold.
Send them on middle passages into the blues.

Michael Meyerhofer

Lessons of the Flood

After that last time, families learned
to keep an ax or a crowbar in their attic
in case the flood waters rose so far,

inch by inch through windows and
doors, up carpeted stairs that children
once slid down by hugging pillows

to their bare chests, just in case
even the attic doors sagged like those
of some cabin in a sinking vessel,

so that families could bust through
their own roof, climb out and
wave for helicopters to rescue them.

Imagine drowning in your attic.
Imagine watching your own downtown
gurgle with tetanus-ridden flotsam

amid disregarded prayers to FEMA,
hearing they rescued Fats Domino
to show their concern for black people.

They say that Noah invented alcohol
because he could not bear the sight
of so much ruin, so much sodden death.

But I am tired of feeling distracted.
We have been left too long on the cross,
even our hearts are splintered now.

So here is the champagne of assassins.
And here, a kayak for your backyard.
And here, an antique called forgiveness.

Is for, to Hold

I didn't tell the water it was a pitchfork.
I believe the water believed it was a trident
on account of the family resemblance.
The road had disappeared, the field,
the sundial was about to go under, meaning shadows
would have been unable to stay on schedule.
When I touched the water with the pitchfork,
it stopped rising, and for a week, an ocean
lived in the valley. Birds landed on the ocean
like this is what an ocean is for, to hold.
A few trees went by and a For Sale sign,
I called the number, how much to buy
this ocean? The pitchfork
had only turned over leaves and banana-peels
into compost. I let it sit with us
at the table, fed it bratwurst and jaw breakers.
During the last flood, someone died
down the way, someone is always dying
when living is called for. We are not fish,
goes the saying, anymore. My neighbor,
who lost his house, says it'll be awhile
before he can stare a glass of water in the face.
We are mostly water, mostly rain, people drown
in themselves. The ocean's a river again
and back where it sleeps. In the middle,
a refrigerator's a new island
of cool & white. I wade into the music of caress
and open the door, let water out into water,
it swims away, everything swims away,
as the river nudges me, follow.

Continuous Revelation to Peter Cooley in Post Katrina New Orleans

Please not now, I said, and he shook his head.
It won't be today, that's all I can say.
Then the dream, which was holding me, let go.
I started falling, the fall to last years,
I pray, but descending I'm holding on.
This morning is one of my small landings.

Here, in the only world I've ever known
(except for paradise I've seen moments
the seconds it revealed itself to me
too bright to see, disguised as sun or moon)
here in New Orleans I will take my stand
next to the invisible, always here,
always beside me when I choose to look,
sometimes disguised as someone small as me.

For Katrina, with Love

Katrina, we feel for you,
You who are blamed for being so heartless.
You huffed and puffed, like a child's nightmare,
And blew our houses down, drowned our people,
Destroyed cities, our very foundations,
And unearthed dreams long deferred.

Of course you had no choice. Called from on high,
You found our high ground wanting.
If we seemed unprepared for your call,
You simply must forgive us.
In the time leading up to your visit,
We were busy waging wars of our own,
Wars in which "We don't do bodycounts."*
So we're just like you, really.
(I'm assuming you don't count, either.)
We're both reluctant avengers,
Which is why I feel for you. We both
Understand the lonely, God-fearing task
Of delivering Freedom. You too know
That people must be freed,
Divested of their homes, pets, possessions,
Made to see nothing lasts, not even masks.
We cannot abide more grins and lies.

If we had spent money on the levees,
If we had not filled acres of wetlands,
If we had not ignored the rising heat,
We may never have known the full pleasure
Of making your worldly acquaintance,
Never known the liberating joy
Of losing our friends, our rights, our culture
In order that we may begin again.

---

* U.S. General Tommy Franks' reply to questions about the numbers of
Afghan and Iraqi dead.

We will rebuild and drinketh of the golden cup
At a Senator's new house on the bay.
We'll drink to you, Katrina,
To your breezy, deep-lunged beauty,
To a dream no longer deferred,
To your pure white skin and depthless blue eyes.

The Rest of the Forgotten

for Midnight, Mississippi, my birthplace

Midnight is a faded general store, a towering cotton
gin, and a Baptist church. Shotgun shacks are scattered
along streets built for horsedrawn wagons, with their
peeling paint and aged façades planted between ancient
cotton fields.

For years we waited for better jobs, decent housing,
good schools. Salvation wore an army uniform. Even
in the height of the cotton industry we didn't earn much,
our weathered hands worked in cotton fields for $5.15
an hour. That was before Katrina. Since the storm
we have to compete with thousands of evacuees,

driving from Alabama, Louisiana, the Gulf shore, into the Delta
arriving here at the end of a last tank of gas. Statistics say we live
below the poverty line. We share what we have with the most
needy, praying to God that it's enough. A talisman for the poor
is giving to keep the reaper from your neighbor's door.

Sunrise Blues

A trumpet apologizes to the air
that will be brown with flies once day heats up,
even unflooded streets heavy with dump.
Blues horn stumbling through regrets.
Last chances. Daybreak.

Time to walk the empty square and seed the sky
with breadcrumbs. The only breeze
what the birds stir up in tight airborne circles.
Gold-specked wings all sun-reflecting swell
and curve around a lady faithful to appetite.

Until the bread runs out. Dawn settles in.
Lady losing coo and whirl, her day is over.
City sounds down to one trumpet holding on
to a blue note and bird scratch on stone.

God knows good omens won't undo spoilage
or bring back trade. Still, there are signs:
bird lady eyes tomorrow morning,
blues man gets a second wind, horn telling
the story behind the eyes, feel-good birds
beneath the stab and swallow,
loose as a neighborhood bar crowd,
trumpet brimming royal blue.

A white-haired man on roller skates
rounds St. Louie's corner on a high note
ruffling the air with startled birds—
Quarter coming back.

Jo LeCoeur

The Source of Nightmare

It is not the blind man wading toward sound
chest-deep in water backed up through sewage,
city deep in bayou where silent moccasin breathe
and gator drag down floating meat.

Not the abandoned one we're coming back for
water rising tonight tomorrow night higher
next night reaching for our minds.

And it is not the child
exactly. Days waiting to get out, holding on
to the smelly white dog, holding on close
among worn down, hungry people.

What tears at us is instinct,
the whimper we hold inside our chests,
no dogs allowed on the bus, child-voice
crying so hard it vomits still sobbing hoarse.

Wading blind toward sound, chest-deep
in lies we tell ourselves to buy back childhood,
new pup, new place to sleep only confirm
the one that matters
lost.

Caesura

Katrina,
Your breath can't blow out birthday candles,
And can't even scatter the dandelion dander;
Your sighs don't fog up any windowpanes,
Don't shake the leaves of trees or novels,
Much less tear the letters from a page.

Katrina, poems might as well be made of bricks,
For all the strength you've got to knock them down:
You're a big, bad wolf, only used to straw and sticks.

Katrina, I'm going to rename you Caesura,
Three syllables that amount to a pause for breath,
Your name no more than a comma or equator,
No longer and no louder than a moment's hesitation,
No greater a disturbance in our city's rhythm.

Cold Hard Facts in the Midst of Swirl

On the star strewn beach
of Lake Quinault
carved by the slow force
of an ancient glacier
thousands of years
before the temperate rainforest's
entangled vast green
held fast along its edges
beneath the startling
aching beauty of the swirling
Milky Way
my only son leans to me
and whispers some
cold hard facts

He says in the center of the galaxy
original stars churn hydrogen to helium
suns like ours live fusing helium
to carbon, neon, oxygen
tapping energy
from the center of the star
at iron the fire burns out
as if doused in water
and a cold dead star
collapses into hollow space

I have a friend in DC
whose problems
rotate around the perfection of
cold white marble
for an immaculate remodeled kitchen
with crisp white cabinets
and Venetian marble
for the downstairs bath
the contractor has made

an error
thousands of dollars
worth of agonizing decisions

That takes place in a universe
of a different sort
Here cold hard facts
came nature made
in the guise of whirling dervishes
cycloped giants
of an over-warmed Gulf
transformed homes
peopled with lives and memories
into misshapen sludge
stench beyond odor
flooded furniture
heaped with blackened mold
rooms rearranged in some
crazy extreme makeover

Friends lost homes
an enchanted city lost its people
pets became packs of starving dogs
Mad Max came to pass in less than 3 days

The wheeling alchemy of two hurricanes
laid bare truths stronger than
iron, marble, and the force of raging water

There is nothing to hold onto
The only thing worth giving is your heart
That which is most alive is hidden deep within.

Kemmer Anderson

After Katrina: A Prayer

Come Jesus, walk across the water again
above sewage, flotsam, and pollution.
Through your Spirit bring us absolution
to heal the broken souls that looted in

the name of greed and anarchy of gun
fire mirroring citizens so undone
by war. How we need to confess our sin
hiding behind the walls of omission.

When the floods lifted up their voice, our screams
for help landed deaf on water and winds
with a roaring of broken levees and dreams
sweeping away history, homes, and friends.

Send out your servants who are not afraid
to tread in your footsteps above the flood
waters that tried to drown God's voice who made
the earth and saved us through a cross of blood.

Linda Back McKay

Moving Life

There is a glass of water on a table.
The eye is drawn from glass
to reflection of glass and back again.

Meanwhile sky, keeper of horizons,
blueblack earth blanket, holds the whole
bowl of a city in its lap.

In the midst of this still
life, a woman ties her
hair with a red

bandana and boils water in a tin
pail while the cracked
mirror hangs crazy.

Finally, after sky parlays with stars,
the city is frothy again
with charcoal, river fish, jazz riffs.

It is a harmonious cat and dog song,
a gumbo of reflections,
as water is life and life is passion.

Ron Paul Salutsky

When the Waters Fall

    we'll don plastic masks
        raise our dead
            onto platforms
                to be hauled
                    to limepits
                        on the outskirts

we'll arrange our hands
        as in prayer,
            form from red
                clay mud the vague
                    shapes of makeshift headstones

when the waters fall
        we'll hide our eyes
            with our hands
                as we search for our homes
                  and those who call us
                    refugees will be forced
                      to meet us
                          in the streets

of oily
      death
         growing cess
            unforgiven levees
            and we'll see that the rain
                has no conscience in falling
                  but we'll bless its attempts
                    to wipe the vagrant seaweed

and pondscum
        and sin of inaction
            from uprooted streets

Joanne Lowery

After Katrina

Put a blender into a fishtank,
press high, then pull the plug,
watch things settle,
the little castle slump on its side.

Everything you put in there
still is. The plastic palm
had its wings cut,
but you can find the pieces.

The marbles and sand lie
in different swells and swirls.
Get used to the new look.
Be like the goldfish

going back and forth
all day among bubbles.
Your world is your world.
Don't be put off by algae

or sludge, the surprise coiled
inside an upside-down clay pot.
Snails will clean up the living room,
mold adds a message

to the picture of Jesus
askew on the bedroom wall.
The kitchen needed a good cleaning anyhow.
Jesus will crawl out of his frame

to help you tidy up.
It was just water with additives.
It only got as high as the tenth stair.
When you cry, little miracles of air

and your August utility bill
find a way to the surface.

Solstice: After Katrina

The doe drinks from Jordan Pond
flicks her futile white flag of surrender
or peace bounds up the snowy bench
of hillside into a rondelet of woods
little heart-hooves reflecting the moment.
A cardinal splashes red whistles
from the highest cedar branch and
earth pauses to catch its breath.

Why am I so sad with this
music all around me?

Banked stones burn with feathers and
a skeleton of porch chimes jingles out
a few hopeful notes but it's not the song
I came to sing. The green wind groans
at a single goose flying low over cynical waters.
The gutshot rabbit in its tangle of briar vein
expects no miracles. I lean against a spindly sycamore
under a conflict of clouds and slurred sun listening

to an eloquent but insane anthem of bruised
blessings so much like the anarchy of love.

Mark Jarman

To a Brainy Child in Distress

Dear mind, suffering far away,
I am writing to you on the other side of the earth.

Belovéd thinker, dwelling on no thought
But pain and the pain of thinking, of the mind,

My mind is on you now. My thoughts,
Lit by a dawn you will not see for hours,

Are with you in your darkness, far away.
I hope it is the darkness of deep sleep,

Dear mind. Belovéd thinker, I hope you wake
Far from estranging trouble, home again

To a good thought, a changed mind.

Survivor at rest

Raw curbs
brittle as bone
amber floods of gravel
red eyes lock thunder
in a yard full of decay
restless hands ache
guided by God
you sing
hymns inside stone

the wind sweeps in circles
showers the uprooted kitchen floor
with breath of dust
shards from earth's collarbone

in your house of broken light
the sun leans west
fire clings to trees, flickers
hard against bare stone

you rest, unafraid of storms
no music, just rain
and thunder growing

Lee Herrick

A Thousand Saxophones

After Hurricane Katrina—A Poem for the
Living and the Dead

You can live by the water and still die of thirst.
I said you can live by the water and still die of thirst
or the worst nightmare come true:
that body of water taking over the bodies.
Sometime, tonight, see which echoes most—
a whisper or a scream. Make it something beautiful,
like, *We will endure* or *Yes, I love you*. Sometime,
tonight, think of water—how it purifies or terrifies,
cleanses, gives and takes away—think how fast
some things can rise—water, fear, the intensity of a prayer.
Officials in New Orleans said they want to save the living.
I hope they do. But I hope they can also honor the dead.
On Bourbon Street, over 3,000 musicians employed
on any given day. Last night, before I fell asleep,
I imagined what a thousand saxophones
would sound like if they all played together—
one thousand saxophones, different songs,
different tempos, Dixieland, Miles Davis.
Maybe it would sound like birds or bombs,
planes or preachers praising the Word
on a hot Sunday and the congregation saying *Amen*,
some people whispering it, some people screaming it.
Maybe it would sound like lightning tearing
open the sky or a thousand books slammed shut after
a horrible conclusion, or a thousand children crying for their
mothers or fathers. Last night, I thought, how far
would a thousand saxophones echo from New Orleans or Biloxi?
Would we hear them in Fresno? Could we imagine the sound?
Could Baton Rouge? Could Washington, D.C.?
I don't know what I should tell you.
But I feel like the saints are marching.
They are singing a slow, deep, and beautiful song,
waiting for us to join in.